Treasures of Gilcrease

GILCREASE MUSEUM
TULSA, OKLAHOMA

GILCREASE MUSEUM

1400 North Gilcrease Museum Road Tulsa, Oklahoma 74127-2100
International Standard Book Number 0-9725657-1-X
Second impression 2005

DESIGN, EDITING, AND MANUFACTURING SUPERVISION: Carol Haralson
PHOTOGRAPHY OF ARTWORKS: Shane Culpepper

PAGES ONE AND SEVEN: Woody Crumbo, *Peyote Bird,* 0227.341

PAGE TWO: Acee Blue Eagle, *Woman Hoeing Corn,* 0227.430

PAGE SIX: Edward S. Curtis, *At the Water's Edge—Piegan,* 4327.969.12
This photogravure is plate 195 from portfolio 6 of the monumental work for which Edward Curtis is
remembered—*The North American Indian,* published in limited edition between 1907 and 1930. The 20
volumes, each with an accompanying portfolio, are organized by tribe and culture area relating to the
Southwest, Great Plains, Great Basin, Plateau Region, California, Pacific Northwest, and Alaska. Collectively,
the works remain one of the most important and controversial portrayals of traditional Native American
culture ever created. Curtis's work, blending art and ethnography, continues to influence the image of
American Indians in popular culture.

PAGE EIGHT: Bert Phillips, *Taos Garden, Phillips Patio,* 0137.529

FRONT COVER/JACKET: Thomas Moran, *Tower Falls,* 0226.1457
Moran saw the Yellowstone region for the first time in the summer of 1871 with the government-sponsored
survey led by geologist Ferdinand V. Hayden. From his loosely sketched and broadly painted field studies of
Yellowstone's unusual landscape, Moran composed highly structured and exquisitely painted watercolors such
as this one, produced in 1872. In a group of works commissioned by his English patron William Blackmore,
Moran managed to convey the feeling of towering waterfalls, vast panoramas, and astonishing geologcial
·formations. He did so by including recognizable elements such as plants and human figures to help establish
scale in his compositions of rarely seen natural wonders. The delicate tints of the watercolor also
approximated the beautiful colors of the unique landscape.

BACK COVER/JACKET: Lakota dress with umbilical case, late 19th century, 84.1795, 1796

Printed in Hong Kong

THIS BOOK IS DEDICATED TO

ROBERT W. AND BRENDA DAVIS,

ROBERT E. AND ROXANA LORTON,

AND RAY H. AND MILANN SIEGFRIED,

WITHOUT WHOSE DETERMINATION, SPONSORSHIP,

AND BENEVOLENCE ITS PUBLICATION

COULD NEVER HAVE OCCURRED.

THESE BENEFACTORS HAVE DEMONSTRATED UNWAVERING

COMMITMENT TO CULTURE AND EDUCATION THROUGH

THEIR INVOLVEMENT AT GILCREASE MUSEUM

AND NUMEROUS OTHER INSTITUTIONS.

THE PEOPLE OF OKLAHOMA ARE PROFOUNDLY THE RICHER

FOR THEIR PARTICIPATION AND PHILANTHROPY.

+

Thomas Gilcrease's Treasure House

BYRON PRICE

C ivilized people generations hence will rise up and call you blessed for what you are doing,"[1] famed Texas author J. Frank Dobie wrote his longtime friend Thomas Gilcrease during the summer of 1950. Dobie had just read an article publicizing the Oklahoma oilman's wide-ranging collecting activities and the new museum he had recently opened in the City of Tulsa to share his unsurpassed collection of rare western Americana with the world.

In the wake of the Great Depression and World War II, Americans from all walks of life were rediscovering the American West. Tourists were pouring into the region, western style clothing and singing cowboys were the rage, and motion pictures with western themes dominated at the box office. Artworks depicting the Old West commanded top prices as well, and competition for masterpieces was keen as collectors entered the market in increasing numbers.

Thomas Gilcrease in the early 1920s.

Such conditions stood in marked contrast to those of the dark, dusty days of the early 1930s, when living artists had struggled for survival and paintings by such renowned western masters as Frederic Remington and Charles M. Russell had often gone begging in the marketplace. Hard times and bargain prices, however, offered unprecedented opportunities for at least a few shrewd collectors with the means to indulge their passion for art.

+

Top, Charles M.
Russell, *On the
Flathead*, 0237.981.
Above, William and
Elizabeth Gilcrease
with their five oldest
children in 1900.
Tom Gilcrease is
standing behind his
father. Right,
Gilcrease with his
brother-in-law Pete
Akers in 1908.

Flush with cash pumped from the oil patch in Oklahoma and Texas, in the 1920s Thomas Gilcrease weathered the Great Depression better than most. He had come a long way from the humble surroundings that had marked his birth in Robeline, Louisiana, in 1890. Tom was the oldest of fourteen children born to William and Elizabeth Gilcrease, a couple of Scotch-Irish, French and Muscogee-Creek Indian ancestry. Soon after his arrival, the Gilcrease family moved to the Creek Nation in Oklahoma Territory where Tom enjoyed a rural childhood and developed an insatiable curiosity about the natural world around him. Raised on the gospel of work, as a boy he helped tend the Gilcrease family's fields and store. Although his formal education was somewhat limited, a love of reading, encouraged by his mother, fostered a lifelong love affair with history, especially that related to American Indians.

Thomas Gilcrease's name was entered on the Creek tribal rolls when he was nine years old, an event with profound future consequences for the youngster. Tribal membership made Gilcrease

eligible for a 160-acre allotment of land, fortuitously located within the famed Glenn Pool oilfield, scene of the first major discovery of petroleum in Oklahoma in 1905. By 1917 more than thirty producing oil wells dotted Gilcrease's property, the income from which had enabled him to further his education at Bacone College in Muskogee, Oklahoma, and at an Emporia, Kansas, teacher's college. Married to Belle Harlow in 1908 and the father of two sons, Tom Gilcrease found the lure of the oil patch irresistible, however, and in 1922 he founded his own exploration company.

Three years later the successful oilman embarked on a trip to Europe that would change his life forever. The journey exposed him to the wealth and grandeur of Old World culture, and it also whetted his appetite for collecting fine art. Although he had acquired his first painting, *Rural Courtship,* a sentimental genre scene by Ridgeway Knight, in Tulsa in 1912, he knew little about art but was eager to learn.

Gilcrease began educating himself in the ways of a collector by haunting galleries and auction houses on periodic trips east and overseas. As a novice in the field, he recognized his limitations and proceeded slowly at first. In time, however, he decided upon an approach that suited both his tastes and his pocketbook. Unmoved by Modernism and

Above, Gilcrease, left, aboard the ocean liner *Olympic* near Holland in the early 1930s.
Left, Ridgeway Knight, *Rural Courtship,* 0126.2352.

Charles M. Russell, *A Doubtful Handshake,* 0237.1450.

knowing that he could not compete with well-established collectors of European masters, Gilcrease embarked on a different, more personal course. He looked to his own heritage for inspiration and resolved to create a collection of fine objects that reflected the breadth of Native American history and culture.

Gilcrease, left, and Robert L. Humber in east Texas at the Allen Tooke No. 2 oil lease in the mid 1930s.

At the time Gilcrease began his quest, the collecting of western American art on a large scale was still in its infancy with only a few significant private or corporate collections in existence. The Atchison, Topeka and Santa Fe Railway had begun one of the first in 1903, acquiring compelling paintings of the Southwest to help advertise the picturesque region to train-traveling tourists. By the 1920s, a few private collectors, including New Jersey stock broker Malcolm S. Mackay, Texas businessman William C. Hogg, and Oklahoma oilman Frank Phillips, were actively buying art of the American West. Phillips, a founder of the famed Phillips Petroleum Company, had even established a private museum to house an increasing array of western art, cowboy gear, Indian artifacts, natural history specimens, and firearms.

DesCygne Gilcrease Denney with her father Thomas Gilcrease looking at the Charles Banks Wilson portrait of Gilcrease in January 1959.

Motivated by a personal appreciation for the works they acquired, such collectors ignored 20th-century art critics, who declared the western genre too illustrative to qualify as fine art, and emerging Modernists, who shunned realism and considered the tenets of the National Academy of Design outdated. Like many other Americans, these collectors eagerly embraced the art of the West and the narrative that underlay it. To Thomas Gilcrease and others of his ilk, artworks with western themes expressed the heart of the American Dream and the national character. On a more personal level, such paintings and sculpture not only imparted a comforting sense of place but also embodied an attractive philosophy of life that embraced rugged individualism, resolute courage, and willing sacrifice.

During the early 1930s, Gilcrease made steady, if not spectacular, additions to his collection, which eventually broadened to include books, manuscripts, and artifacts as well as art. Although his oil business had flourished in the previous decade, Gilcrease's marriage to Belle Harlow had not, and in 1926 the couple divorced. Two years later, the entrepreneur married Norma Smallwood, a former Miss America. The second union produced a daughter, but within a few years this union also failed.

In 1937 Gilcrease moved his company headquarters to San Antonio, Texas, to be closer to his major field operations. Thereafter he became more active as a collector and in 1942 formed the Thomas Gilcrease Foundation, in part to facilitate his ongoing collecting interests, but also to support such philanthropic efforts as Indian education. The following year he acted on a long held desire to establish a museum where he could exhibit his treasures for the public. Art historians generally consider this display, located at Gilcrease's company headquarters in San Antonio, to be the first museum ever devoted to western American art.

The opening of the Thomas Gilcrease Collection in the ballroom of a former supper club foreshadowed a string of remarkable acquisitions that would vault its founder to the forefront of western Americana collectors by the end of the decade. The first of these, the purchase of Dr. Philip G. Cole's incomparable western art collection in 1944, was also the most important. Between 1919 and his death in 1941, Cole, a tire magnate who had spent his childhood in Montana, filled his New York mansion with more than 500 works by such important artistic interpreters of the West as Frederic Remington, Charles M. Russell, Charles Schreyvogel, and Frank Tenney Johnson. The $250,000 asking price for the collection, however, stretched even Gilcrease's substantial resources and required him to pay the bill in four installments over a three-year period. Widely regarded as the single greatest acquisition of western art of all time, the transaction netted the Oklahoman some 636 works of art as well as books, photographs, and associated archival material.

Above, the Thomas Gilcrease Museum in San Antonio in 1945. Right, the study of Philip Cole's New York estate.

Gilcrease conducted his careful negotiations for the Cole collection under a veil of secrecy. By mutual agreement the transaction was not made public for two years. Competition for western masterworks, especially those created by Frederic Remington and Charles M. Russell, had become more intense by the 1940s, and before the Cole coup Gilcrease's collecting activities had been overshadowed by others. The most active of the Oklahoman's several well-heeled challengers were Texans led by Fort Worth newspaper publisher and oilman Amon G. Carter, who had begun to collect western painting and sculpture with vigor in 1935. Thanks in part to the influence of Oklahoma humorist Will Rogers, Carter and his colleagues, Sid Richardson, a Fort Worth entrepreneur with oil and cattle interests, and C. R Smith of Dallas, named president of American Airlines in the late 1930s, developed a special interest in the art of Charles M. Russell. Smith, for example, purchased half of Russell's estate in 1940, leaving the remainder to another oil company executive, Charles S. Jones. Richardson and Carter also acquired significant works by the Montana cowboy artist, although Carter's landmark acquisition of Sid Willis's famous Mint Saloon collection did not occur until 1952. Thomas Gilcrease, who had acquired forty-six

paintings and twenty-seven bronzes by Russell as part of the Philip Cole collection, appreciated the legendary artist's narrative approach to his work and especially valued his sensitive handling of Native American subject matter.

Although their collecting rivalry was sometimes spirited, Gilcrease and his Texas colleagues remained cordial and, at times, even helpful to one another. As one art scholar has observed, they "admired each other's abilities and realized they shared a common love for the West."[2]

After completing the Cole purchase, Gilcrease's collecting quickened at a dizzying pace. In 1948 alone, the collector landed several major prizes,

among them the estate of noted landscape painter Thomas Moran. The acquisition included some 2,000 works of art, including many exquisite watercolors of the Yellowstone region of Montana and Wyoming, and also archival material that helped reveal Moran's creative process. That same year Gilcrease completed negotiations for the purchase of an important collection of art and correspondence of George Catlin, the first artist to travel extensively among the tribal peoples of the American West. He also snapped up several romantic depictions of the American fur trade and Plains Indian life painted in the 1830s by Alfred Jacob Miller. To many knowledgeable observers, however, Gilcrease's 1947 purchase of Thomas Eakins's magnificent full-length portrait of famed ethnologist Frank Hamilton Cushing for a surprisingly small sum overshadowed them all. Art dealer William F. Davidson called the historic transaction "the greatest single acquisition in Western and perhaps American art history. . . "[3]

Alfred Jacob Miller,

Fort Laramie,

0126.727.

Gilcrease far outpaced his contemporaries not only in sheer number of acquisitions but also in the breadth and elasticity of his collecting vision. Besides securing stunning artworks, the Oklahoman bought thousands of rare books, manuscripts, and documents, including certified copies of the U. S. Declaration of Independence and of the Articles of Confederation. An interest in the Spanish and Mexican influence on American history led him to acquire more than 100,000 pages of Hispanic source material, some of it dating from the 16th century. This important cache of the written word included documents related not only to such famous explorers and conquistadores as Christopher Columbus, Hernán Cortéz, and Hernando de Soto, but also to the Spanish Inquisition in the Americas.

Thomas Gilcrease's unparalleled success in securing so many important collections in such a short time did not depend solely upon his substantial financial resources, although a strong wartime demand for petroleum had significantly augmented his fortune. Luck also played a part, as did an intricate network of business and personal relationships with some of the most renowned art and book dealers in the United States and Europe. Because Gilcrease was not the only collector in the field, timely access to important potential acquisitions was critical, and connections with such insiders as Daniel B. Browne, Victor D. Spark, and William F. Davidson, and with such art houses as M. Knoedler & Company and Stendahl Galleries, among others, were a must. In 1943 Gilcrease hired Martin Wiesendanger away from Kennedy Galleries in New York to become the first director of his new San Antonio museum.

Contemporaries often described Thomas Gilcrease as a man of principle and sound business judgment. His taciturn demeanor, sometimes difficult for others to read, belied a keen, if dry, sense of humor that served him well in sometimes prolonged negotiations with gallery owners and booksellers. A sharp dealer with an intuitive sense of value, he seldom found himself at disadvantage in a trade. Yet he would often pay a premium for objects that especially interested him.

To Gilcrease the content of an artwork sometimes counted for more than its aesthetic attributes. Despite developing a discriminating eye for quality, the Oklahoman sometimes acquired paintings with limited visual appeal provided they were historically significant. A different impulse led him to collect distinguished works outside his declared areas of interest. The acquisition of noteworthy paintings by such prominent American artists as Winslow Homer, John Singer Sargent, and James McNeill Whistler reflected this tendency and lent both breadth and context to the western American focus of his collection.

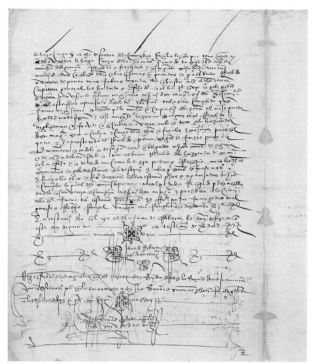

Signed decree by Hernán Cortéz, 4075.3916.

Below, John Singer Sargent, *On the Coast of Brittany*, 0126.2254.

An engaged and interactive collector, Tom Gilcrease took great pleasure in reading and discussing the books and manuscripts he acquired, took an active part in the archaeological excavations he sponsored, and enjoyed the company of artists he admired. On periodic forays to the famous artists' colony at Taos, New Mexico, for example, Gilcrease developed friendships with and purchased paintings directly from several artists, including Ernest Blumenschein and Bert Phillips. He acquired some 200 works from the prolific Joseph Sharp alone, not to mention the fine collection of Indian artifacts the artist had gathered over the years for use as props in his work. The letters the pair exchanged between visits indicate the genuine fondness and warmth the artist and his patron felt for one another. Gilcrease also extended his encouragement and support to promising young Native American artists, collecting and commissioning work by Acee Blue Eagle, Woody Crumbo, and Willard Stone, among others.

Gilcrease left, with Acee Blue Eagle, center, and Willard Stone. Below, Ernest L. Blumenschein, *Ranchos Church with Indians,* 0137.2195.

Despite Gilcrease's spectacular achievements as a collector in the 1940s, San Antonians never mustered much enthusiasm for his museum. Disappointed by their apathy, the founder closed the display in 1947, after only a few years of operation. The distractions of World War II and its aftermath, coupled with the exhibit's downtown corporate location and perhaps a general lack of community awareness, contributed to its demise.

Undeterred by his failure in Texas, Gilcrease moved his collection back to Tulsa where he placed it in a new museum adjacent to his own modest sandstone home west of downtown. The founder opened the new facility, called the Thomas Gilcrease Museum, in May 1949.

Joseph Henry Sharp, *Leaf Down at the Studio Door*, 0137.349.

Although he continued to collect at a torrid pace, the oil revenues that Gilcrease depended upon to finance his acquisitions began to lag thanks to overproduction, declining prices, and government regulation. By 1953 the overextended collector found himself financially strapped and unable to pay some $2.25 million he owed to business associates and to galleries and art brokers for various acquisitions.

As the beleaguered oilman began to look for a way out of his difficulties, several suitors for his collection emerged. Institutions of higher education, including the universities of Texas, Oklahoma, and North Carolina, expressed interest, as did the Will Rogers Memorial at nearby Claremore, Oklahoma. So did Amon Carter, who wanted to establish

his own western art museum in honor of Charles M. Russell and Will Rogers at Fort Worth. Meanwhile, an opportune feature story in the March 8, 1954, issue of *Life* magazine and another in *Time* raised national awareness of Thomas Gilcrease's remarkable collection and its uncertain future.

To fend off the entrées of competitors, the City of Tulsa organized a successful bond issue in 1954, designed to pay the oilman's debts and to secure his treasures for the community. Gilcrease transferred title to his collection the following year, and the museum was renamed the Thomas Gilcrease Institute of American History and Art. In 1958 the founder deeded the museum buildings to the community, along with more than thirteen acres of land. He had already assigned the city a half interest in several mineral leases to protect its interests while the bonds were being repaid.

Despite his financial travails, Gilcrease never lost his passion for collecting or for his collection. As his economic position improved in the late 1950s, he continued to acquire rare western Americana, although the field became increasingly crowded with eager collectors. An ongoing fascination with archaeology and ethnology also led him to sponsor several field excavations of Indian mounds in the Mississippi Valley. The objects acquired from his digs and his other post-1955 collecting efforts eventually reached the museum through a bequest after Gilcrease's death from a heart attack in May 1962.

Although the indefatigable collector did not live to see the countless other gifts, donations, and improvements that enabled his museum to grow and flourish into the new millennium, by every measure Thomas Gilcrease realized his long held desire to leave a mark on the world. The museum that bears both his name and his spirit now, as during Gilcrease's lifetime, houses the largest collection of western American art ever assembled, more than 10,000 works in all. The shelves of its library accommodate some 100,000 rare books, manuscripts, and other archival material, much of it unique, and its galleries and vaults display and store a quarter million extraordinary artifacts related to the aboriginal people of the Americas.

American art historian Richard Saunders once called the Gilcrease Museum "a kind of Smithsonian Institution of the American West."[4] Although a powerful tribute, Saunders's comment only hints at the museum's ongoing impact and influence. No mere static display, the collection that Thomas Gilcrease built is today at the very forefront of a fresh, vigorous, and ongoing debate over the meaning of the West in American history and art. Its art and artifacts are in constant demand for prestigious national and international exhibitions and by academics engaged in primary research on various subjects. An authoritative book about the art of the Old West can hardly be written without reference to its holdings.

At the turn of the 21st century, scholars construe the American West very differently from the way their colleagues viewed it a few decades earlier, when Tom Gilcrease's collecting activities were at their peak. The perspective of today's New Western historians is more diverse but often darker than that of their antecedents, and the theme of loss has largely replaced the theme of progress as their guiding interpretive principal. Likewise, the art of the American West is no longer viewed as simple historical analogue but rather as a potent, complex, and symbol-laden product of Manifest Destiny and myth. By collecting, preserving, and honoring the material culture of indigenous peoples, by encouraging contemporary Native American artists, and by actively embracing his own Indian heritage, Thomas Gilcrease was, in many ways, a man ahead of his time. That he resolutely and successfully pursued his goals, yet avoided the pessimism, rancor, and rhetoric that often characterize the current pursuit of western history, is a tribute to the maturity and breadth of his vision.

This book only samples the visual and intellectual feast that is the Gilcrease Museum today. No single volume could ever do justice to the magnificence of the collection or to the lifetime of interest and effort of the collector who assembled it. Yet the individual objects that grace the pages that follow are carefully chosen representatives of the whole. Some are iconographic, others anonymous. Most are rare, aesthetic, and historic, and all have stories to tell. Interwoven, however, these individual threads form a sturdy, variegated, if sometimes soiled, tapestry of America's western experience.

1 Quoted in David R. Milsten, *Thomas Gilcrease* (San Antonio: Naylor, 1969): 342.

2 Richard H. Saunders, *Collecting the West: The C. R. Smith Collection of Western American Art* (Austin: University of Texas Press, 1988): 49.

3 Quoted in Dean Krakel, *Adventures in Western Art* (Kansas City: Lowell Press, 1977), 27.

4 Saunders, *Collecting the West*, 50.

The Fine Arts Collection

ANNE MORAND

During thirty years of collecting, Thomas Gilcrease acquired over 10,000 paintings, drawings, sculptures, and prints. His fine art collection makes up the smallest segment of the vast holdings of the Gilcrease Museum, which includes major groups of historical and anthropological objects as well. Demonstrating his interest in material that illustrates, documents, and embodies the varied aspects of American culture, the collection also represents Gilcrease's own view of American history and his tastes.

The fine art collection at Gilcrease is a survey of American art history, focusing on 400 years of representational art. The people, activities, and landscapes of America are depicted in styles ranging from Colonial and Neoclassical to Romantic and Modernist by America's most distinguished artists. This book, while limited to a select few examples, offers an introduction to this eminent collection.

Typical of the committed collector, Thomas Gilcrease put his collection together in various ways. Almost certainly he envisioned the end result as a museum, and he worked to acquire important pieces that would reveal the many aspects of the nation's growth. So Gilcrease instinctively followed the primary method of most collectors: to develop a direction or plan and then work to implement it. And, with income from oil revenues, he had the resources to back up his aspirations.

Although Gilcrease began collecting in the 1920s, some of his most significant artworks were not acquired until the late 1940s and early 1950s. Working with prominent galleries and dealers, such as M. Knoedler & Company, Victor D. Spark, and Kennedy Galleries in New York, he sought out fine examples by artists outstanding in the American canon. From Knoedler came Thomas Eakins's *Frank Hamilton Cushing*, Winslow Homer's *Watching the Breakers*, James McNeill Whistler's *Nocturne, the Solent*, John James Audubon's *The Wild Turkey*, John Singleton Copley's *Portrait of Mrs. John Apthorp, née Hannah Greenleaf*, and Charles Willson Peale's *James Madison*. Knoedler was also responsible for bringing to Gilcrease's attention the availability of the Thomas Moran studio collection of nearly 2,000 works, exemplified by the stunning *Shoshone Falls on the Snake River*. Kennedy Galleries provided Albert Bierstadt's beautiful *Sierra Nevada Morning*, and Victor Spark sold Gilcrease Charles Deas's *Siouxs Playing Ball*, Jasper Cropsey's *View on Lake George*, and John Singer Sargent's *Arrival of the American Troops at the Front*.

A private dealer, Daniel B. Browne, alerted Thomas Gilcrease to an opportunity that expanded the already significant museum collection with 800 pieces of western art. Gilcrease purchased the Philip G. Cole estate, which included such outstanding paintings as Frederic Remington's *Indian Warfare*, Charles M. Russell's *Carson's Men*, Charles Schreyvogel's *Breaking Through the Line*, and Frank Tenney Johnson's *California or Oregon*. Prior to this acquisition in 1944, the Gilcrease collection included none of the western art for which it is so well known today.

One of the characteristics of the Gilcrease fine art collection that enhances its unique quality is breadth within sub-collections. The Moran collection, for example, includes not only finished work, but also sketches, prints, letters, ledgers, and ephemera. Another example of an extensive assemblage is the work of George Catlin, acquired from the English bibliophile Sir Thomas Phillipps through the efforts of dealer William Robinson, Ltd. Hundreds of oils, watercolors, lithographs, and letters make this one of the largest groups of Catlin material in any single institution. Clearly, Gilcrease saw the importance of supportive material that enhanced our understanding of an artist's career and working process.

Gilcrease also gathered the art and documentary material of several other artists. Alfred Jacob Miller's *Sir William Drummond Stewart Meeting Indian Chief* is one of a number of Miller oils and watercolors he acquired from various Miller heirs. He bought directly from Joseph Henry Sharp more than half of

the artist's over 400 paintings now at Gilcrease Museum. Sharp collected Indian artifacts, and several of the ones featured in *Crucita — Taos Indian Girl in Old Hopi Wedding Dress and Dried Flowers* are also now in the Gilcrease collection. Gilcrease's rapport with living artists is revealed by direct acquisitions of Bert Phillips's *The Corn Maidens* and Ernest Blumenschein's *Superstition*. The artists knew that Gilcrease was developing a world-class collection and each held in reserve for him some of their most important works.

A detail from *Crucita — Taos Indian Girl in Old Hopi Wedding Dress* by Joseph Henry Sharp. Below, objects Sharp used for the painting which were acquired by Gilcrease.

The appeal of the Gilcrease fine art collection is appreciated nationally, evidenced by the number of people from throughout the country who visit it annually. The inclusion of works from the collection in numerous critically acclaimed exhibitions demonstrates their importance to the history of American art. The Eakins and Whistler traveled to exhibitions in New York, Paris, and London. The Moran and Bierstadt were featured in Washington, D.C. The Sharp and Blumenschein were showcased in a significant exhibition dedicated to the artists of Taos, New Mexico.

Yet the greatest significance of Gilcrease Museum is, as its founder envisioned, that in the heart of America an outstanding collection of materials relating to the country and hemisphere exists for the entertainment and enlightenment of the public.

JOHN COTTON (1693-1757) was minister of the Newton, Massachusetts, Church when this portrait was painted. He graduated from Harvard in 1710 and was ordained as minister of the Church at Newton in 1714. Cotton came from a long line of religious leaders, the first a Puritan minister who arrived in New England as part of the Great Migration. The Cotton family flourished so that during the colonial period there were at least six men named John Cotton. The family also included Cotton Mather, the Puritan clergyman, scholar and author.

Smibert was the first European painter of merit to immigrate to the colonies, and he found a successful society eager for portraits. He brought with him not only the tradition and style, but also the craft, of European painting. His studio was a place where young artists could gather and see the work of a professionally trained painter.

+

JOHN SMIBERT English, 1688-1751
PORTRAIT OF JOHN COTTON, ca. 1735
Oil on canvas, 0126.1004

26

HANNAH GREENLEAF (1744-1773) was a member of a prominent Boston family and married into a comparable social position. She is portrayed wearing a modest hairstyle and no facial adornment, which was prohibited by religious attitudes of the day. Her clothing reveals the prosperity of colonial families and the proficiency of period painting. The exquisite rendering of textures, delicate hues, highlights, and shadows accounts for much of the portrait's aesthetic appeal. The dark background focuses attention on the subject's face, and her plain features are imbued with a dignity that reveals her composure and the security of her place in society.

Portraiture abounded in the American colonies in the 1750s and 1760s. Copley, America's first native-born master, stands out among his peers. He learned the basics of painting from his stepfather, Peter Pelham (c. 1695-1751), a Boston painter and engraver. Two itinerant English painters brought the popular Rococo style to Copley's attention, along with methods for depicting beautiful silks and satins. The ability to render these textures, combined with Copley's talent for capturing the character of a sitter, made him extremely popular among art patrons. He received the most sought-after portrait commissions of the time. His sitters were of a certain social or intellectual world that saw the role of a portrait as a statement of status. They often had their portraits made to document the acquisition of wealth, a change in upward social status, or, as in this case, marriage.

✢

JOHN SINGLETON COPLEY American, 1737-1815
PORTRAIT OF MRS. JOHN APTHORP, NÉE HANNAH GREENLEAF, 1765
Oil on canvas, 0126.1012

Following many years of intermittent war, peace between the Cherokee Nation and Great Britain was ratified in 1762. The Cherokee king, or commander-in-chief, Cunne Shote journeyed with two subordinate leaders from the Carolinas to England aboard a British frigate, H.M.S. *Epreuve*, to sign treaties. The London press noted that "Three Cherokee Indian Chiefs arrived in London from South Carolina. They are well-made men, near six feet high, well dressed in their own country habit, with only a shirt, trousers and mantle round them; their faces are painted of a copper colour, and their heads adorned with shells, feathers, ear-rings and other ornaments. They neither of them can speak to be understood, and very unfortunately lost their interpreter on their passage." The chiefs were presented to George III, who received them graciously at the Court of St. James.

Parsons, a leading portrait painter of the day and a member of the Incorporated Society of Artists of Great Britain, was commissioned to paint this portrait. Called a kit-cat, which means a three-quarter-length portrait with hands showing, it represents Cunne Shote wearing two medals. The silver one shows the heads of George III and Queen Charlotte, and the gold one is inscribed "Entirely English 1762." Along with a silver gorget, marked "G.R.III," the medals were gifts from the king.

+

FRANCIS PARSONS English, ?-1804
CUNNE SHOTE, CHEROKEE CHIEF, 1762
Oil on canvas, 0176.1015

28

THE SUBJECT OF THIS PORTRAIT, whose name was actually Ostenaco, was a member of the delegation of three Cherokee leaders who traveled to England in 1762. Because of the death of their interpreter, there was much confusion, even concerning names and titles, during their stay in England. This portrait, however, is particularly significant; never before had an identifiable American Indian been painted on such a large scale, or in such a regal and imposing manner.

Reynolds, the leading portrait painter and court painter to George III, painted Ostenaco as an ambassador from the wilderness in a costume significant of his past and of his present connection with the English. This portrait reveals many of the aspects of Reynolds's work that made him popular. Although Ostenaco was nearly sixty, he is portrayed as ageless. In an effort to achieve his own perception of physical beauty, Reynolds omitted aspects of personal adornment that he did not understand or appreciate aesthetically: Ostenaco was heavily tattooed and his earlobes were slit and stretched to enormous size (in 18th-century England, large earlobes were a sign of underlying irrationality). Reynolds required three sittings of ninety minutes each to complete the portrait. During the sittings, he concentrated on the head and hand, finishing draperies and background without the sitter present.

+

JOSHUA REYNOLDS English, 1723/1792
SCYACUST UKAH, 1762
Oil on canvas, 0176.1017

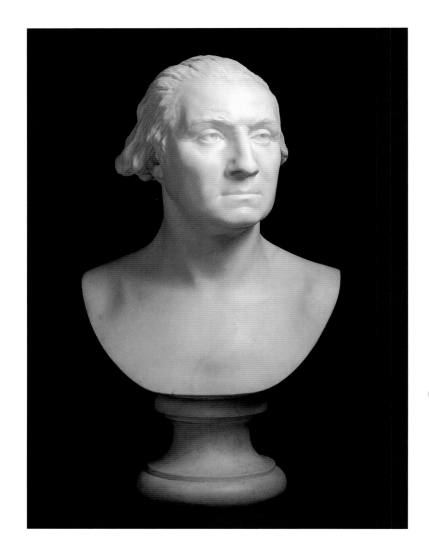

AT THE CLOSE of the Revolutionary War, the state of Virginia voted to erect a statue of George Washington (1732–1799). Thomas Jefferson and Benjamin Franklin arranged for Jean Antoine Houdon, the most important sculptor of the Neoclassical period in Europe, to receive the commission. Pleased with the honor, he volunteered to journey to Virginia to meet Washington instead of working from a painting. Franklin accompanied Houdon on his voyage from France to Washington's home, Mount Vernon, in the fall of 1785. After making sketches and clay models from sittings and taking a life cast, Houdon returned to France to complete the life-size, full-figure marble. He also carved many busts of Washington based on his original sittings.

In 1775 Washington moved into international prominence as commander-in-chief of the American forces. Washington's military reputation was established during the French and Indian War, and Congress unanimously commissioned him to lead the Continental Army. Washington came to his post with an understanding of the technical side of his command. In a war of defense, he was patient and prudent in the use of his forces. He also displayed imagination in daring undertakings that served to maintain American spirit. Yet perhaps Washington's most important attribute during the war years was his fidelity to the revolution. He inspired others through his devotion to the cause of republican liberty.

Several years after completing his bust of Washington, Houdon began work on the first of two portraits of the Marquis de Lafayette (1757–1834). Considered by the French to be Houdon's masterpiece, the Gilcrease portrait shows the revolutionary hero in the uniform of commander of the guard. Lafayette, though a wealthy idealist and member of the French aristocracy, was an enthusiastic supporter of liberty. He came to the American colonies in 1777 aboard a ship equipped at his own expense to help the American cause. Congress commissioned him a major general in the Continental Army just before his twentieth birthday, and Washington gave him a small independent command in 1777. After distinguishing himself in battle, Lafayette's greatest service was political. In 1779, while on a mission home, he persuaded King Louis XVI of France to send out an expeditionary force to North America. Under the command of Comte de Rochambeau, the French troops helped Washington win the decisive battle of Yorktown.

+

JEAN ANTOINE HOUDON French, 1741–1828
GEORGE WASHINGTON, 1788
Serravezza marble, 0976.4
GENERAL LAFAYETTE, 1789
Serravezza marble, 0976.3

Washington, best remembered as the first president of the United States and commander of the Continental Army during the American Revolution, began his career of public service twenty years earlier. He served as a member of the Virginia House of Burgesses, as a justice of Fairfax County, as a delegate to the First and Second Continental Congresses, and as the president of the Philadelphia Convention at which the Constitution was written.

Among Peale's portraits of statesmen, *James Madison* is particularly remarkable. Painted fourteen years before Madison (1751‑1836) was elected the fourth president of the United States, it commemorates his role as the "father of the Constitution." Peale exhibited this painting in his Museum Gallery in Philadelphia, where Madison was named to the Board of Visitors in 1792, along with Thomas Jefferson and other prominent men. Peale believed his portraits served the national interest and felt the men he portrayed were visual

ONE OF THE TRUE EMBODIMENTS OF ENLIGHTENMENT in America was Charles Willson Peale. Based on his belief that proper training could create expertise, Peale began one of the first art schools in America, the Columbianum Academy (now the Pennsylvania Academy of the Fine Arts) in Philadelphia. His own training, however, by necessity came from formal study in London with Benjamin West (1738‑1820), from whom he learned a sophisticated portrait style.

Peale painted George Washington (1732‑1799) from life seven times between 1772 and 1795, eventually producing sixty portraits. Well known to colonial leaders, Peale was a captain in the American Revolution and was involved in the Battles of Trenton and Princeton. He served on several military and civil committees and in 1779 was elected a Philadelphia representative to the General Assembly of Pennsylvania. John Adams wrote, "Peale is from Maryland, a tender, soft, affectionate creature. He is ingenious. He has vanity, loves finery, wears a sword, gold lace, speaks French, is capable of friendship, and strong family attachments and natural affections."

embodiments of republican ideals. *James Madison* is part of a series of portraits painted for his gallery in a simple Neoclassical style on the assumption that the sitters' virtues were apparent in their physical features. Writing to Jefferson, Peale explained, "I love the art of painting, but the greatest merit of execution on subjects that have not a virtuous tendency lose all their value in my estimation."

Madison's record of public service was impressive. He was a member of the Continental Congress, the Annapolis and Philadelphia Conventions, and the U. S. House of Representatives as well as serving as secretary of state. One of the most brilliant American political thinkers of the era, Madison was a leader in the development of the first ten amendments to the Constitution known as the Bill of Rights.

+

CHARLES WILLSON PEALE American, 1741‑1827
PORTRAIT OF GEORGE WASHINGTON, 1795
Oil on canvas, 0126.1013
JAMES MADISON, 1792
Oil on canvas, 0126.1006

WILLIAM TEMPLE FRANKLIN (1760–1823) was the son of William Franklin and the grandson of Benjamin Franklin. He was the elder Franklin's secretary at the 1783 Peace of Paris, which concluded the American Revolutionary War. During the early 1770s, young Franklin provided a link between his father and grandfather. The father, who was in the British army and served as royal governor of New Jersey, never supported American independence. In 1782 he left his native country permanently. Even after the war, William and Benjamin met only once and never reconciled. William Temple Franklin was often his grandfather's companion and seemed content to be a man of leisure in Europe and America. His grandfather secured his election into the American Philosophical Society in 1786, but was not successful in attaining a congressional appointment for him.

Brown painted this portrait in Paris in 1791, when the young Franklin was editing his grandfather's writings. Brown had met the Franklins in Paris in 1781, when he came to Europe to pursue artistic training. Benjamin wrote letters of introduction for the painter, as did William Temple, saying "Permit me to introduce to your acquaintance the Bearer Mr. Brown, a Young Gentleman from America, who proposes residing sometime in London with a View of perfectioning himself in the Art of Miniature painting – He is a Young Man of good Family & of a very amiable Character: and I shall esteem as done to myself any Civilities you may think fit to shew him." Brown became one of most successful and sought-after portraitists in England and France.

+

MATHER BROWN American, 1761–1831
WILLIAM TEMPLE FRANKLIN, 1791
Oil on canvas, 0176.1016

VANDERLYN is the best representative of Neoclassical art in America, as well as one of its few practitioners. Extensive training in Paris under instructors such as Jacques Louis David (1748-1825) gave him a solid grounding in the ideals of a period in European art and politics that drew upon ancient Greece and Rome for its inspiration. His grand historical narratives won him praise and substantial rewards in Paris, including the gold medal from Napoleon.

Vanderlyn returned home to America in 1815 hoping to create heroic images based on Revolutionary subjects. Instead, he found an art climate that was not conducive to the creation of major history paintings. The government, still recovering from its arduous birth, was not prepared to patronize artists on the scale typical in Europe. The only type of painting still lucrative in America was portraiture, but Vanderlyn refused, with the scorn of the Neoclassicists

who considered portraiture beneath them, to support himself in this manner until it was obvious he would never receive government patronage.

His American masterpiece, *Washington and Lafayette at the Battle of Brandywine,* painted at least a generation after the actual battle, is indisputable evidence of his ability as a painter. The mastery of draftsmanship and form so important to the success of Neoclassical painting is combined with elements taken directly from the ancient Greeks. The principal figures and the horses are carefully drawn composites of figures found on the west frieze of the Parthenon and the "Alexander" sarcophagus, both dating to about the fourth century B.C. The two generals represent the enlightened man in America, composed in a symbolic language that is foreign today, but that was easily understood within the context of the classic ideals of the new republic.

+

JOHN VANDERLYN American, 1775-1825
WASHINGTON AND LAFAYETTE AT THE BATTLE OF BRANDYWINE
Oil on canvas, 0126.1018

ALTHOUGH KING WAS A WELL-TRAINED ARTIST, it was the fact that he was a gregarious, witty man that allowed him to become part of Washington society, which in turn opened doors for many important commissions. There he met Thomas L. McKenney, the representative of the Office of Indian Trade, who was responsible for the important body of work King left for posterity. More than 100 portraits representing more than twenty tribes were painted for the government under McKenney's sponsorship from 1821 to 1842.

Indian leaders were scheduled for portrait sittings with King while in Washington. Among these was Mak-Hos-Kah, who came to the capital to negotiate treaties and trade agreements. King also painted Mak-Hos-Kah's wife, Rent-Che-Was-Me, who accompanied him on the trip. Attention to details of clothing and personal adornment makes King's work a valuable ethnographic as well as aesthetic contribution.

✦

CHARLES BIRD KING American, 1785-1862
MAK-HOS-KAH, CHIEF OF THE GOWAYS, 1825
Oil on panel, 0126.1198
RENT-CHE-WAS-ME, MAK-HOS-KAH'S WIFE (FEMALE FLYING PIGEON), detail, 1825
Oil on panel, 0126.1202

nt·che·was·me, Mak·hos·kah's Wife.
(Female Flying Pigeon.)

SULLY, one of the most prominent portrait painters in America, began his career in Philadelphia in 1801. Returning to his native England in 1809, he studied the work of Benjamin West (1738–1820), Sir Thomas Lawrence (1769–1830), and Sir Joshua Reynolds (1723–1792), whose influences can be seen in the elegant, aristocrat bearing of his subjects and the painterly quality of his execution. After his return to the United States, he settled in Philadelphia, then the art center of the country, and quickly found success. His following grew so strong and his work obtained such vogue that he was called on to paint Philadelphia's loveliest women and most distinguished men. Acknowledged as a rapid and industrious painter, Sully is known to have completed over 2,000 portraits and more than 500 subject paintings.

Perhaps his most eminent sitter was Charles Carroll (1737–1832), who signed the Declaration of Independence for the colony of Maryland and outlived all the other signers. Carroll is remembered also as a Revolutionary leader and as a

United States senator from Maryland. As a Catholic, he was disenfranchised under English law, yet he became increasingly active in the Revolutionary effort and was elected a Maryland delegate to the Continental Congress in July 1776. From this time on, he took a prominent part in the Maryland Assembly and the Continental Congress. In 1787 he supported the adoption of the Constitution of the United States.

Sully began this portrait of the elderly statesman with four days of sittings in Baltimore in May 1826, making elaborate oil studies and sketches and returning to Philadelphia to complete the full-length work. Compare Sully's portrayal with a contemporary written description of Carroll, and it is easy to understand one of the factors in Sully's great popularity—his ability to accurately record, yet flatter, his subjects. Carroll was described as "Below middle size, weak and emaciated. His hair was scant and white and silky, and his eyes especially were suggestive of great age."

+

THOMAS SULLY American, born England, 1783–1872
CHARLES CARROLL OF CARROLLTON, 1827
Oil on canvas, 0126.1019

JARVIS, the nephew of the English Methodist preacher John Wesley, was born in England and brought to Philadelphia as a child. Showing promise as an artist, he was apprenticed to a painter/wood engraver, one of the typical training methods for artists in the 19th century. During his apprenticeship, Jarvis began painting portraits and miniatures, eventually becoming one of the most popular portrait painters from New York to New Orleans.

A year before he suffered a paralyzing stroke that ended his career, Jarvis painted this striking double portrait of Black Hawk (1767–1838), the noted chief of the Sauk tribe, and his son Whirling Thunder. It reflects Jarvis's mature style, characterized by the use of dramatic highlights and painterly brushwork. The two Sauks sat for Jarvis in Washington, where President Andrew Jackson brought them in 1833.

Many Indians supported the British during the Revolutionary War and the War of 1812. Throughout these years, warfare continued as tribes fought against encroachment into their homelands. One such episode, which became known as the Black Hawk War, was a fifteen-week event in 1832, during which Black Hawk and his followers refused to relinquish ancestral lands. Following several encounters, the Massacre at Bad Axe ended Indian resistance in the Old Northwest. Black Hawk and other leaders surrendered at Prairie du Chien. President Andrew Jackson summoned a group of six, including Black Hawk and his eldest son Whirling Thunder, to Washington after their imprisonment in Illinois territory. The group was held at Fort Monroe from April until June 1833 and then returned to the frontier by way of the principal eastern cities—Baltimore, Philadelphia, and New York—to be impressed by the power of the United States. From the time the journey began, the Indian prisoners were celebrities and tourists. Jackson, as it happened, was also touring the eastern seaboard cities along a parallel route; both Jackson and Black Hawk drew great attention and comparison in the press.

+

JOHN WESLEY JARVIS American, born England, 1780–1839
BLACK HAWK AND HIS SON WHIRLING THUNDER, 1833
Oil on canvas, 0126.1007

39

WILLIAM DRUMMOND STEWART (1795–1871), a wealthy Scottish nobleman, first visited the American West in 1833. A gentleman-sportsman, he came in search of adventure and recreation; hunting big game in the West provided both. He made several trips west, and in 1837 joined a supply caravan headed for the Green River Rendezvous in present-day Wyoming. Traveling with an entourage of his own, Stewart was accompanied by numerous people, including a valet, a chef, and, most interestingly, an artist—Alfred Jacob Miller.

Miller, a Baltimore-born, European-trained artist, had met Stewart in 1837. A product of Enlightenment thinking that saw the Indian as the noble savage and the American wilderness as the Garden of Eden, Miller quickly grasped the importance of the invitation to join Stewart's associates. During that single summer, Miller made hundreds of

sketches, such as *Mirage on the Prairie*, of the Indians, the events, and the landscape. Miller, as one of the earliest known artists to see and paint the Rocky Mountains and the Far West, was the only artist to sketch firsthand the annual rendezvous of the white and Indian fur traders. Just a few years after his visit, the fur trade all but ceased.

Stewart's route, which came to be known as the Oregon Trail, provided Miller with ideas and inspiration that he would use for the rest of his career. Many of the paintings Miller made upon his return to his Baltimore studio, such as *Indians on Green River*, celebrated the remote beauty of the far West. *Sir William Drummond Stewart Meeting Indian Chief* is an unusual and striking portrait of Miller's patron.

+

ALFRED JACOB MILLER American, 1810–1874
SIR WILLIAM DRUMMOND STEWART MEETING INDIAN CHIEF, ca. 1840s
Oil on canvas, 0126.738

INDIANS ON GREEN RIVER, ca. 1840s
Oil on canvas, 0236.732
MIRAGE ON THE PRAIRIE, 1837
Watercolor on paper, 0236

41

WITH AN APTITUDE FOR ART and an interest in the natural world, Audubon capitalized on the fascination with birds that was ubiquitous in 19th-century Europe and America. He traveled the southeastern United States tracking and killing bird specimens he would then wire into lifelike poses in his studio. Audubon published *Birds of America,* a multi-volume set that included 1,065 life-sized illustrations. The wild turkey was one of the largest species represented.

This oil painting is a replica Audubon made of the first plate in his *Birds of America.* Although he painted it twenty years after the original watercolor, it is identical in composition and detail.

+

ALTHOUGH DEAS HAD PREPARED to enter military service, he did not, opting instead for formal art training at the National Academy of Design. In Philadelphia Deas saw an exhibition of George Catlin's Indian paintings and determined to see the West for himself. Visiting his brother at Fort Crawford, he began to collect scenes of Indian life, an activity that would engage him for a decade. Works such as *Siouxs Playing Ball* were popular due not only to his style as an artist but also to the desirability in the East of subjects such as games and hunting.

+

CHARLES DEAS American, 1818/1868
SIOUXS PLAYING BALL, 1843
Oil on canvas, 0126.1152

CATLIN was the first artist to travel to the interior of the continent specifically to paint and record the native cultures he encountered. He made hundreds of sketches on which paintings such as *The Bear Dance* were based. Complex in composition, this work includes numerous figures, fully developed special relationships, and rich color. The painting depicts a dance of the Western Sioux in preparation for a bear hunt. Individuals are shown dressed in masks representing the bear and in attitudes that mimic the movements of the animal. Paintings including *The Bear Dance* were toured through the eastern United States and then to London and Paris as part of Catlin's Indian Gallery. His work received critical acclaim in Europe, and the exotic material intrigued audiences and some artists for several years. The majority of Catlin's collection ended up in the Smithsonian Institution, but not until the artist had died, dispirited

because of his own government's lack of interest in native cultures. Catlin foresaw the end of many traditional Indian ways and worked all his life to leave an accurate record of the lives of those he called "Nature's noblemen."

Catlin also recorded scenes of places important to native life. He described a source of steatite as the "Pipestone Quarry, on the Coteau des Prairies, 300 miles N.W. from the Falls of St. Anthony, on the divide between the St. Peter's and the Missouri. The place where the Indians get the stone for all their red pipes. The mineral, red steatite, variety differing from any other known locality—wall of solid, compact quartz, grey and rose colour, highly polished as if vitrified; the wall is two miles in length and thirty feet high, with a beautiful cascade leaping from its top into a basin. On the Prairie, at the base of the wall, the pipeclay (steatite) is dug up at two and three feet depth."

+

GEORGE CATLIN American, 1796-1872

BEAR DANCE, 1847

Oil on canvas, 0126.2171

PIPESTONE QUARRY, COTEAU DES PRAIRIES, 1848

Oil on canvas, 0176.2168

CATLIN wrote about Mah-To-Toh-Pa in *Letters and Notes:* "This extraordinary man, though second in office is undoubtedly the first and most popular man in the nation. Free, generous, elegant and gentlemanly in his deportment— handsome, brave and valiant. . . . He took his attitude before me, and with the sternness of a Brutus and the stillness of a statue, he stood until the darkness of night broke upon the solitary stillness. His dress, which was a very splendid one, consisted of a shirt or tunic, leggings, moccasins, lance, tobacco-sack, and pipe; robe, belt, and knife; medicine-bag, tomahawk, and war-club."

Catlin Painting Mah-To-Toh-Pa, 1847, a pen and ink drawing from The Catlin Sketchbook, 4776.6.66.

+

GEORGE CATLIN American, 1796-1872
MAH-TO-TOH-PA, THE FOUR BEARS, 1847
Watercolor on paper, 0226.1543

RANNEY PAINTED WESTERN HISTORY, GENRE, and scenes of the Revolutionary War. His best and most popular works were those focusing on the often-dramatic stories of the pioneers. Born in Connecticut, Ranney spent part of his youth in North Carolina before moving to New York to study art. During those impressionable years, he must have heard stories of heroes such as Daniel Boone that stayed with him. *Boone's First View of Kentucky* was painted at least fifteen years after Ranney returned to the North. It received contemporary critical acclaim as one of his best paintings and gained him election as an associate member of the National Academy of Design in 1850.

Although most of Ranney's paintings are set out of doors, like nearly every other artist of the time he painted in the studio. This enabled him to control all aspects of the painting, such as light and the poses of the figures. Ranney,

who did not know Boone, may have relied for details on books such as *Life of Daniel Boone* by John M. Peck, published in 1847. The accoutrements in *Boone's First View of Kentucky* coincide remarkably with Peck's descriptions of Boone and his fellow travelers John Finley, John Stewart, Joseph Holden, James Monay, and William Cool, who were described as wearing a "hunting shirt, or loose drawers of the same material, covered the lower extremities, to which was appended a pair of moccasins for the feet. The cape or collar of the hunting shirt, and the seams of the leggins were adorned with fringes... A leathern belt encircled the tomahawk, to be used as a hatchet; on the right side was the hunting-knife, powder-horn, bullet pouch, and other appendages indispensable for a hunter. Each person bore his trusty rifle..."

WHISTLER'S placid *Nocturne, the Solent* is now considered a masterpiece but it elicited negative reaction from late 19th-century public and critics when it was first shown. Whistler's work is avant-garde in its Modernism, ignoring Impressionism's preoccupation with sunlight. His nocturnes were attempts to paint the way night is: distances are negated; colors are subdued or disappear into a hazy blue (which he strove diligently to create out of paint pigment); perspective and clearly defined planes cease to exist.

Massachusetts born, Whistler received his early art education at West Point but was dismissed before completion of his studies. Leaving America permanently in 1855, he traveled to Europe to study the masters, finally establishing studios in London and Paris. He began a lucrative career painting admirable portraits, but it was landscape he loved. At first he painted subdued tonal landscapes in which the subject was not as important as the execution. As he turned away from the literal, critics and the public could not easily

+

JAMES ABBOTT MCNEILL WHISTLER American, 1834-1903
NOCTURNE, THE SOLENT, 1866
Oil on canvas, 0176.1185

follow. The Victorian art public wanted paintings that were "windows," framing scenes they could understand. Whistler, who wanted the public to realize that paintings were flat surfaces made of paint, was heralding trends to come. A lack of definition in his subjects, a refusal to follow accepted technical procedures for mixing and applying paint, and a disregard for traditional composition demonstrate Whistler's desire to create surface rhythms and effects independent of narrative. Oriental prints, which had been imported from Japan, revealed the possibilities of calm, simple compositions, reduced to essential elements.

This work resulted from the artist's trip to Chile aboard the *Solent*. Painted on an almost monochromatic surface that he manipulated with a brush to suggest water, the ship and two others are barely discernible. After a critic equated one of his paintings to a musical work, Whistler began using titles such as Nocturne, Symphony, Arrangement. He is recognized as an artist who led the way to 20th-century artistic freedom.

BIERSTADT introduced Americans to the power and majesty of the landscape of the Far West. His success as an interpreter of the region came from a combination of influences. From his German academic training he learned the importance of structure in composition, meticulous workmanship, and exquisite color. Early exposure to the best of the Hudson River School painters, such as Thomas Cole and Frederic Church, convinced him of the importance of landscape as a subject. Therefore, when Bierstadt traveled west in 1859 with General Frederick Lander's army expedition, he was artistically and philosophically prepared to take advantage of the experience. His paintings, visual essays on the stunning western terrain, appealed enormously to eastern audiences and critics and demonstrated the Hudson River School's predilection for the epic vision, the panoramic view, and the outsized canvas.

The Sierra Nevada range in California provided inspiration for majestic images such as the imaginative *Sierra Nevada Morning*. Based on various sites Bierstadt visited, the painting is a composite rather than a portrait of one specific place, revealing the tendency of the romantic painter to improve upon nature. Bierstadt, who did not pretend to be profound, was content to be a popular picture maker who could package the sublime for common consumption.

After a trip to the coast of California and the Farallone Islands near San Francisco, Bierstadt began a series of exquisite seascapes. These paintings, which include *Point Lobos, California*, reveal a strength of Bierstadt's not seen in his mountain landscapes. Sunlight glows through translucent water breaking against a glistening shore or against jagged rocks and shimmers off the drenched coat of resting seals.

+

CROPSEY WAS ONE OF THE MOST POPULAR PAINTERS of the Hudson River School, as well as one of its finest draftsmen. His early work shows the effect of influential painters Asher B. Durand (1796-1886) and Thomas Cole (1801-48). Cole especially affected Cropsey's rich handling of paint. By the 1850s the artist had developed his characteristic style—warm, autumnal landscapes painted in a crisp and realistic manner. Once refined, this style was retained throughout his career.

Although Cropsey trained as an architect in New York, a lack of commissions turned him to painting. He studied at the prestigious National Academy of Design, becoming a member in 1851, and exhibited there regularly. Fortunately for him, painting proved more lucrative than architecture. Burgeoning tourism demanded beautiful landscapes as souvenirs and Cropsey began painting familiar views of the White and Catskill Mountains and the Hudson River to satisfy this need. He also made extended trips to Europe before settling permanently in Hastings-on-Hudson, New York, in 1864.

View on Lake George is typical of Cropsey's mature style. The amiable, realistic autumnal scene of placid water and friendly wilderness demonstrates why his work was so popular.

+

JASPER FRANCIS CROPSEY American, 1823-1900
VIEW ON LAKE GEORGE, 1874
Oil on canvas, 0126.2316

THE CIVIL WAR disillusioned the American public about the future of the unspoiled natural world. Coincidentally, there was also a lessening of interest in the American style and a rapidly growing interest in the more fashionable French. Inness's work was popular because in his later career he successfully bridged the gap between America and Europe.

Inness was first active in the mode common to the Hudson River School painters, which included sharply focused, realistically painted landscape. However, travel in Europe and exposure to the effects of the Barbizon school and to the Impressionists elicited a change in his style. *A Windy Day* exemplifies the changes Inness's work underwent. He incorporated elements from European art that suited him, such as the rich color and the interest in mood from the Barbizons and the soft focus from the Impressionists, and combined them with his own strong response to nature. In

his later period he moved even farther away from literal depictions of nature to a style rich with atmosphere. Many of his paintings give the viewer the impression of wind, rain, and cloudy skies in late evening or early morning. Typically, with Inness, there is no thrashing, stormy landscape, but instead a gentle day to which has come an afternoon shower and, later, clearing. *A Windy Day* documents the first steps of Inness's dematerialization of fact.

Inness received praise for his work, which he exhibited regularly at the National Academy of Design after becoming a member in 1869. His soft brushwork, his technique of dissolving outline in glazes of rich color, and his fluid paint application are technical developments unique to Inness. Although some of these characteristics are similar to those of the Impressionists, Inness was not interested as they were in the fleeting effects of light, in an impression of the moment.

+

GEORGE INNESS American, 1825–1894

A WINDY DAY, 1883

Oil on board, 1883, 0126.2260

TRAINED IN THE PARIS ACADEMIC SYSTEM that stressed draftsmanship and composition, Brush was one of the most classically trained artists to approach American western subjects. His Indian subjects are highly sophisticated, as seen in the poignant *Mourning Her Brave*, and show his interest not only in the romantic aspects of the Indian but in the factual information—facial features and artifact details are so accurate they can be identified historically and anthropologically. Considered the best of all his Indian pictures, *Mourning Her Brave* clearly emphasizes the spiritual aspect of life and projects a feeling of desolation of landscape and spirit, a haunting tale of aloneness. In this composition of a grieving woman silhouetted against a snowy cliff that holds the body of her mate, Brush shows himself to be a painter more of mood than action. The Indian mourner is self-absorbed, her thoughts concentrated inward.

+

GEORGE DE FOREST BRUSH American, 1855-1941
MOURNING HER BRAVE, 1883
Oil on panel, 0126.1189

WATCHING THE BREAKERS is part of a series of spectacular seascapes that Homer painted at Prout's Neck, Maine, between 1890 and 1910. Paintings such as *Watching the Breakers* were part of a continuing tradition in which landscape painters sought new impulse and inspiration, the last vestiges of wilderness in an increasingly tamed land. His contemporaries considered these seascapes his greatest achievement, prompting Thomas Eakins to call him the greatest painter of the era. Much of the force of his great oils of the 1890s comes from his vigorous brushwork, controlled somber palette, and strong design structure.

Homer, born in Boston, was trained as a wood engraver, and his first work was to provide illustrations of soldiers' activities during the Civil War. After the war Homer began his career as a fine artist, painting men and women in everyday pursuits, hunting, fishing, school teaching, and at leisure. The last three decades of Homer's life were the most creative, and from the 1890s came the greatest number of his masterpieces. Almost every year of that decade produced clusters of memorable images, many inspired by Prout's Neck, a rocky peninsula about ten miles south of Portland. Homer bought land and built a residence there in 1882, first spending summers, but eventually living there full-time.

Literary and social critics have observed the general impulse toward the end of the 19th century to deify women. *Watching the Breakers* reveals stately women set against an exploding sea; it embodies the timeless values of womanhood, such as calm in the face of all adversity.

+

WINSLOW HOMER American, 1836-1910
WATCHING THE BREAKERS, 1891
Oil on canvas, 0126.2264

MORAN, a late product of the Romantic period, was in his element among the strange and wonderful landscapes of the Far West. Beginning with images of Yellowstone, Yosemite, and Grand Canyon in the 1870s, Moran spent the rest of his career documenting the beauties of the American scene. Competent and strong, his work was suited to the majesty of the subjects depicted.

Although Moran painted until the end of his life, *Shoshone Falls on the Snake River* was his last heroic-sized canvas. Painted as a memorial to the "Western Niagara" that would soon cease to exist in its natural form due to damming of the river, Shoshone Falls may also be seen as a protest against the destruction of the wilderness.

Scenes of the American West were not Moran's sole subjects. Many more of his paintings depicted eastern America, Mexico, and the British Isles. A rare, intricate, large format watercolor, *Pass at Glencoe, Scotland* resulted from Moran's visit in 1882. Responding to the horrific history of the site where the Macdonalds were massacred at the hands of the Campbells in 1692, Moran has represented a melancholy and starkly beautiful landscape. The brooding composition is rich with such details as a horse-drawn coach and a man herding cattle across the Three Rivers Bridge; tiny sheep are spread over the hillside while the river is strewn with Moran's characteristic rocks.

THOMAS MORAN American, born England, 1837-1926
SHOSHONE FALLS ON THE SNAKE RIVER, 1900
Oil on canvas, 0126.2339
PASS AT GLENCOE, SCOTLAND, 1882
Watercolor on paper, 0226.1656

CHASE was one of the most respected and versatile American artists of his time. He painted portraits, interiors, landscapes, and still lifes with an unsurpassed mastery of color, composition, and technique. Executed in a bravura style that paid homage to European masters such as Frans Hals (1580?/1666) and Diego Velasquez (1599/1660), Chase's work reveals extensive training at such important schools as the National Academy of Design in New York and the Royal Academy in Munich. Until Chase began exhibiting still lifes, the genre was considered a student exercise. With his mastery of texture and form, he elevated simple compositions to works of great appeal.

While in Munich, Chase earned such esteem as a teacher that he was offered a position at the Royal Academy. He opted to return to New York to teach at the newly formed Art Students League. Dividing his time for the rest of his life between the League and the Pennsylvania Academy of the Fine Arts, Chase later established his own summer school at Shinnecock, New York. There he insisted that students paint out of doors, and many of his seaside paintings were demonstration pieces. The quality of the light and the immediacy of the scene were things he hoped his students would value. This small Long Island town where Chase spent the summers with his children was also a haven away from the frenetic pace of New York City. Chase's daughters were often featured in paintings such as *Shell Beach at Shinnecock*.

+

WILLIAM MERRITT CHASE American, 1849/1916
SHELL BEACH AT SHINNECOCK, AFTER 1892
Oil on canvas, 0126.2252
STILL LIFE
Oil on canvas, 0126.225

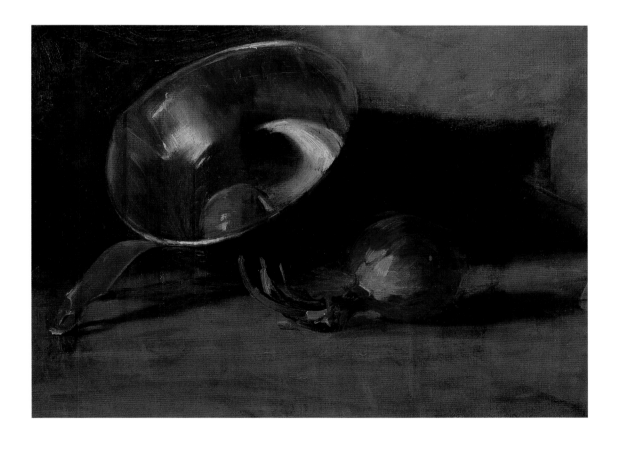

THIS PAINTING of Frank Hamilton Cushing is doubly impressive—both for its artist and its sitter. Cushing, whose most noteworthy accomplishment was his fieldwork among the Zuni Indians of the Southwest, was the first anthropologist to live among the people he investigated. His "participant-observer" methods yielded unprecedented information. Eakins built a career painting exceptional portraits of distinguished men and women. The Cushing portrait was Eakins's first full-length, life-sized male portrait. Together, the artist and anthropologist constructed a model of a Pueblo room in Eakins's studio, which is seen in the background of the portrait. Eakins worked on the portrait for several months, making sketches and photographs to work from when Cushing was not available to pose. Cushing also loaned Eakins the clothing and objects included in the composition so that they could be rendered accurately.

+

THOMAS EAKINS American, 1844-1916
FRANK HAMILTON CUSHING, 1895
Oil on canvas, 0126.2315

The Arrival of the American Troops at the Front is a
remarkable painting, considering that Sargent painted it in
the midst of the chaos of troop movements. Hired by the
British government to create murals commemorating the
cooperation between American and British troops, Sargent
traveled to France to make his studies. The immediacy of the
work is its strength, evident in the brisk, bravura brushwork,
the dazzling light, the lack of minutia, and the evocation of a
sensory response. The road is choked not only with people,
ambulances, and animals, but also dust that is palpable. With
these elements Sargent also implies a cacophony of voices,
machinery, and artillery fire to which the viewer relates on an
emotional level.

+

JOHN SINGER SARGENT American, born Italy, 1859-1925
THE ARRIVAL OF THE AMERICAN TROOPS AT THE FRONT, 1918
Oil on canvas, 0176.1219

A CONTEMPORARY OF FREDERIC REMINGTON (1861-1909) and Charles Russell (1864-1926), Farny concentrated his efforts on depictions of daily life of Plains Indians. He differed from his contemporaries in his extensive training, received in the academic tradition in Rome, Dusseldorf, Vienna, Munich, and, briefly, Paris. The influence of northern Europe is seen in Farny's interest in detailed genre subjects in tightly constructed compositions. A master draftsman, Farny brought sophistication of technique to western painting.

Born in the French Alsace, he was brought to America as a child. Farny's parents, who left France to escape religious and political oppression, settled in a sparsely populated part of western Pennsylvania and later relocated to Cincinnati. Farny began working as an illustrator to help support the family after his father died. His earliest published work appeared in *Harper's Weekly* in 1865. The next year he moved to New York and soon after left for Europe to study. He returned to Cincinnati in 1870, established his studio, and continued to work as an illustrator until 1890.

Farny traveled in the West and Southwest between 1881 and 1894, concentrating on Indian subjects both in illustration and fine art. *The Sorcerer* and *Fording the Stream* are examples of his mature work, in which he utilized the warm, somber palette of northern Europe to create sympathetic portrayals of Indians. The two paintings reveal distinctly different aspects of Indian life. *Fording the Stream* recounts the migratory nature of Plains life, with the tribe spread out along the riverbank, waiting while a young man tests the safety of the ford. It is an occasion of community activity, while *The Sorcerer* reveals a more private, solitary side of life. A single figure inhabits a nearly empty landscape, emphasizing the introspective nature of worship.

+

HENRY F. FARNY American, born France, 1847-1916
THE SORCERER, 1903
Oil on canvas, 0127.1225
FORDING THE STREAM, 1905
Oil on canvas, 0127.1224

In the American West at the end of the 19th century, most of the open ranges were fenced, and the nomadic Indian tribes were restricted to reservation lands. However, the West of legend continued to thrive in the work of artists and writers. One of the most intriguing is Frederic Remington, who began his career as a western illustrator before moving into the area of fine art.

Remington's boisterous battle between Plains Indian warriors and the U.S. cavalry, *Indian Warfare*, presents action laid out in a frieze of figures that rips across the picture plane. The Impressionistic, broken brush strokes he uses to paint the vibrant, almost unbelievable, palette add to the frenetic energy of the piece. The static cavalry, just visible in the scumbled background, appears to be veiled in the dust kicked up by the Indian ponies. The positioning of the figures, both Indian and horse, enliven the scene even further; one can almost see the group as the stop-action progression of a single figure.

At the time that Remington was changing directions with his paintings, he was also experimenting with three-dimensional work. Bronze was a medium through which Remington could exploit further his love of action and drama. The lost-wax method of casting enabled him to push to the limits the tensile strength of bronze and to create compositions in which figures seem to hang in the air. *The Buffalo Horse*, a masterpiece depicting a grand collision of buffalo, horse, and hunter, seems precariously balanced on the slender back legs of the buffalo.

Creating over twenty subjects in bronze before his death, Remington made multiple castings of most of them, producing more as sales demanded. An exception is *The Buffalo Horse*, of which there is only a single cast. The largest vertical piece that he sculpted, it was considered at the time by the critics and the public to depict too brutal a subject, and therefore did not sell.

+

IN COMPLETE CONTRAST to Remington's scenes of high action is *Hungry Moon*. The cool moonlit setting belies the desperation that drives the Indian women to work late into the cold winter night butchering the buffalo that will feed and clothe their families. Remington began painting what he called "Moonlights" in 1900, and with their exhibition came the favorable critical reviews he had so desperately sought. Based on extensive examination of the moods of night and experiments with painterly effects, works such as *Hungry Moon* revealed Remington's place as an important American modernist. A *New York Times* reviewer commented, "The paintings of night may presage great things for Mr. Remington." Unfortunately, Remington's early death cut short the potential for works of even more significance.

SCHREYVOGEL'S WORK is considered an important record of the interaction between the soldiers of the government and the warriors of the Plains Indians. Although he was working well after the height of the Indian wars, his paintings have a feeling of authenticity due to the thoroughness of his research. Well accepted by both public and critics, his color work and draftsmanship received high praise.

An appealing aspect of Schreyvogel's work was his use of visual tricks to add interest to his compositions. In *Breaking Through the Line*, as with the eyes in some portraits, the aimed gun appears to point at the viewer from any angle. The impact of the painting is further heightened by the action in the immediate foreground, which appears to be pushing out of the picture plane toward the viewer.

CHARLES SCHREYVOGEL American, 1861-1912
BREAKING THROUGH THE LINE, 1903
Oil on canvas, 0127.1235

SELTZER WAS FASCINATED WITH THE WEST and the people who lived there. He settled in Great Falls, Montana, where his artistic outlook was influenced by fellow resident Charles M. Russell (1864-1926). Academic training received in his youth at a training school for the Royal Academy of Copenhagen is evident in the carefully constructed compositions, able brushwork, and vibrant color.

An interest in history made Seltzer invaluable to his patron, Dr. Philip Cole, who wanted to surround himself with memories of the West. Seltzer helped him fulfill this desire. In paintings such as *Prowlers of the Prairie,* Seltzer was recreating historical events, the majority of which had occurred long before his lifetime. Through careful research in conjunction with Cole, he was able to produce authentic paintings that recall a time when Plains Indians freely roamed the western lands.

OLAF CARL SELTZER American, born Denmark, 1877-1959
PROWLERS OF THE PRAIRIE, 1926
Oil on canvas, 0137.899

ONE OF THE GREAT TEACHER-ARTISTS, Henri forms a link between the traditional painters of the 19th century and the radicals of the early 20th. In his early twenties Henri began his formal art training, first at the Pennsylvania Academy of the Fine Arts, then in Paris. For several years he investigated everything from the academics to the Impressionists, then he returned to Philadelphia to begin his career as a teacher. He continued to travel extensively in Europe, changing and modifying his style and methods. He ultimately abandoned Impressionism for the darker toned and broadly brushed styles of Frans Hals (1580?-1666) and Diego Velasquez (1599-1660).

Henri became an advocate of younger artists, encouraging them towards freedom of expression while insisting upon a firm grounding in tradition and technique. Although he was part of the art establishment, he also explored options for less restrictive avenues for the exhibition of younger artists. In 1907 when the work of several of his friends was rejected by

the National Academy, he set up the groundbreaking exhibition *The Eight*. He continued to help organize exhibitions of young, independent artists, culminating with the controversial Armory Show of 1913 that showcased Modernism in America.

Henri traveled extensively in the American Southwest. At the time of his second trip to Santa Fe, New Mexico, in 1917, he began to include native design elements in his portraits and to place more emphasis on the complementary space around his figures. Brightly keyed and boldly patterned geometric textiles were hung behind the models, creating a complex and decorative background design. This is particularly effective in this portrait of Gregorita, featured in a series of large portraits. Henri wrote, "When the model takes her place, the background recedes and exists only as a complement to the figure. All the beauty that can exist in the background rests in its relation to the figure. It is by looking at the figure that you can see this relation."

+

ROBERT HENRI [ROBERT HENRY COZAD] American, 1865-1929
GREGORITA, 1906
Oil on canvas, 1906, 0137.570

69

RUSSELL made the man's world that was the American West his subject. Herding cattle, hunting, warfare, and aspects of the daily life of Plains Indians and Euro-Americans were observed in his paintings. Affection for the heroes of the past resulted in historical and poignant images such as *Carson's Men*. Symbolically, figures representing western entrepreneurs of an earlier period are arrayed against the sunset. Recognized more often for the narrative quality of his work, Russell could also paint compositions of great sensitivity and beauty. The late afternoon sunlight reflected in the water and sky in *Carson's Men* seems to glow with its own life.

Russell had an affinity for three-dimensional art and created numerous bronzes. Most were single animal or human figures, which makes *Counting Coup* one of his most ambitious compositions. Based on a story about Medicine Whip, a Blackfoot warrior, the sculpture celebrates his feat of counting two coups at once against Sioux foes. Counting coup, striking an enemy without necessarily killing him, was considered the epitome of courage and prowess.

CHARLES MARION RUSSELL American, 1864-1926
CARSON'S MEN, 1913
Oil on canvas, 0137.2245
COUNTING COUP, 1907
Bronze, 0837.19

HUMOR was frequently part of Russell's compositions, but in many cases it was a poignant note regarding fate. The hunter has been successful in bringing down a mountain sheep, but it is just out of easy reach, thus the title *Meat's Not Meat 'Til*

It's In the Pan. The hunter's dilemma is of no concern to the horses, patiently waiting. As long as they can forage, they won't go hungry.

+

Perhaps no painter of his time was more thoroughly steeped in academic tradition than Leigh. The years spent in the Munich schools as an art student paid off handsomely in his long and successful career as a western and southwestern painter. Munich meant long, intensive training in draftsmanship, in detail, and in preparation and execution of a composition. For the large format canvases he painted in his New York studio, Leigh made numerous pencil studies, oil sketches, tracings, and other preparatory work. The final canvas, begun with carefully rendered pencil and charcoal underdrawings and finished with intricate paint application and meticulous detail work, took months to complete.

A painting such as *Argument with the Sheriff* was not a quickly painted impression of the West but a story built on canvas as carefully as a writer builds on paper. Leigh's works were often stories meant to enlighten about the ways of men in the West. Here a group of horse thieves is fighting a long battle against the sheriff's posse, unwilling to give up without a struggle. The action and drama are evident not only through dashing brushstroke or play of light and shadow but also through the physical placement of figures caught in a moment of peril (the falling horse), the expressions of faces, and the atmospheric elements such as rising dust.

+

WILLIAM ROBINSON LEIGH American, 1866-1955
ARGUMENT WITH THE SHERIFF, 1912
Oil on canvas, 0127.716

Dramatic, almost melodramatic, *A Close Call* recounts an actual event from the spring of 1912 in Wyoming. Leigh joined a group of hunters hired by the director of the Colorado Museum of Natural History to take a grizzly bear specimen for a habitat group. When, after a lengthy search, a large bear was held at bay by dogs, Leigh sketched quickly before the animal was shot. He later described the scene in his unpublished autobiography as a "quarterless battle raging fast and furiously" where "five dogs encircled a bear who had

cunningly taken to the deep snow, and was standing upright, his back against a large tree, fighting them off."

Leigh used his quick sketches along with oil studies of animals and background elements such as *Cow Creek, Wyoming* to create *A Close Call*. The fallen hunter in danger at the feet of the bear was a fictional aspect Leigh added to heighten the excitement.

+

WILLIAM ROBINSON LEIGH American, 1866–1955
A CLOSE CALL, 1914
Oil on canvas, 0127.2232
COW CREEK, WYOMING, 1910
Oil on canvasboard, 0137.2227

From his childhood home in Iowa on the Overland Trail, Johnson's earliest memories were of settlers going west, memories that served his later artistic career. His paintings have a humanness about them; in *California or Oregon* one can empathize with the protagonist in the throes of decision-making. Where will he find a better life for himself and his family?

Using very painterly brushstrokes, Johnson created vibrant canvases that have a luscious quality unsurpassed in works by any of his contemporaries. He was particularly interested in the effects of light that glowed and shimmered on rocks and on water. His composition was seldom involved with the more active or violent side of the Wild West. Johnson preferred instead to focus on the individual, the internal struggle and dilemma, or on the peaceful although raw beauty of the western landscape.

Artists have been attempting to capture the appearance of night for centuries. Almost a paradox, the idea of painting the lack of daylight requires rejection of the usual definition of visual perception for humans—object illuminated by light. Johnson and others, of course, could not paint completely without illumination, but they instead looked at the mitigating effects of the moon, stars, and firelight. In *The Pony Express* the moon's cool light casts a silvery sheen over the landscape. A counterpoint of firelight through the window of the structure warms the composition. Only artists like Johnson who spent time observing the night could successfully paint it. The choice of night as backdrop for the action of the pony express rider heightens the drama and danger.

✦

FRANK TENNEY JOHNSON American, 1874-1939
CALIFORNIA OR OREGON, 1926
Oil on canvas, 0157.1090
THE PONY EXPRESS, 1924
Oil on canvas, 0127.1088

SHARP VISITED TAOS, NEW MEXICO IN 1893 and became the strongest advocate for adopting the sun-drenched village as an artists' colony. At a time when many artists were fleeing the restrictive atmosphere of the traditional art centers, particularly New York and Philadelphia, many art colonies were founded. Few became so well known as Taos. Artists like Sharp found inspiration there and lived in harmony with the land and the original inhabitants, the Pueblo Indians.

Crucita — a Taos Indian Girl in Old Wedding Dress and Dried Flowers is a contemplative, light-flooded interior portrait of one of Sharp's favorite sitters. It demonstrates the artist's eye for composition, his evocative use of shallow space, his ardent interest in details, and his mastery of textural variation that avoids fussiness in lieu of painterly execution.

Before Sharp visited Taos, he spent a number of years painting near the Crow Agency in Montana. One of the benefits of being there for long periods of time was that he saw the encampments of the Crow at various times of the year and, more importantly, in different lights. Perhaps the first to paint the translucent light glowing through the hide tipi walls, Sharp not only documented the reality but also exploited the unusual beauty of the effect.

+

JOSEPH HENRY SHARP American, 1859-1953
CROW TEEPEES AT NIGHT, 1890s
Oil on canvas, 0137.548
CRUCITA — A TAOS INDIAN GIRL IN OLD WEDDING DRESS AND DRIED FLOWERS, 1926
Oil on canvas, 0137.2194

Couse received excellent training in America and Paris, where he perfected the draftsmanship and classic technique that formed the basis for his long and successful production. One of the Taos group who spent summers working in the Southwest and winters exhibiting in New York, Couse introduced many of America's art patrons to the beauty of the Southwest.

Compositions that focused on a single, often introspective, figure were a Couse specialty. The setting of *The Arrow Maker* is an interior, not as common as Couse's outdoor settings, but strikingly beautiful nonetheless. The radiance of the contemplative mood ennobles a rather ordinary activity in a domestic setting.

+

EANGER IRVING COUSE American, 1886–1936
THE ARROW MAKER
Oil on canvas, 0137.2193

UFER, one of the most unusual and most celebrated of the painters who worked in Taos, New Mexico, in the mid-20th century, studied art first at the Dresden Royal Academy and later at the Royal Academy of Munich. Northern European influence is seen in his expert draftsmanship and use of strong color. After his first visit to Taos, Ufer spent winters in New York and summers in New Mexico before moving permanently to the Southwest. Ufer exhibited at major shows and won coveted prizes and critical acclaim. He was elected a member of the National Academy of Design in 1926.

An ardent socialist, Ufer was concerned with the plight of all he felt to be persecuted. *Hunger* is an odd combination of emotion and acceptance on the part of the subjects. The composition, like many of Ufer's, is energetic, the colors bright and strong. Detail, minimal, and confined to the most important elements, is effective and helps develop the theme.

+

WALTER UFER American, 1876-1936
HUNGER
Oil on canvas, 0137.531

SLOAN'S CAREER centered on his work as an illustrator in New York, but after his first visit to Southwest in 1919, he bought a New Mexico home where he spent summers for the rest of his life. An experimental artist, Sloan created *Indian Art by the Highway* with glazes of color built up over the underpainting to define form and used hachure lines for shading and definition.

Indian Art by the Highway was based on his observations during car trips to the Southwest. Sloan wrote, "The picture with the modern speedway to Albuquerque cutting the desert, and the family resting in the shade, suggests the timeless calm of the Indian in face of the timesaving efforts of modern civilization."

+

JOHN SLOAN American, 1871-1951
INDIAN ART BY THE HIGHWAY, 1937
Oil on board, 0137.568

BLUMENSCHEIN was a well-rounded, articulate artist whose work received international acclaim. Training in Paris acquainted him with the influential French styles of his time and helped him develop ideas about art that he kept throughout his career. In Paris, Blumenschein met fellow student Joseph Henry Sharp (1859/1953), with whom he later formed the Taos Society of Artists. Sharp's encouragement prompted Blumenschein's first visit to Taos and his subsequent decision to establish a studio there.

Although he spent summers in Taos, Blumenschein was active in the New York art society. Works based on his New Mexico experience, such as *Superstition*, won prestigious prizes at the National Academy of Design and brought notoriety to both artist and place. *Superstition*, a complex painting in both design and subject, is indicative of Blumenschein's profound response to Taos. In a passage that sums up his attitude and that of Taos painters in general toward events of Indian life, he wrote: "The Indian's mind is partly 'made up' by medicine men who are often fakers who play on all superstitions that have come into his life—and in addition he has the religion of the white man which he gets from a priest that is not always conscientious. Add to that his own Indian religion in which the beautiful dances are so important, and the result is one more confusing than I can depict in my picture with its vivid colors and shapes.... So I tried to paint the Indian friend's feelings—and maybe my own.... It grew into this picture, which will be interpreted according to the intelligence of the onlooker."

+

ERNEST LEONARD BLUMENSCHEIN American, 1874/1960
SUPERSTITION, CA. 1921
Oil on canvas, 0137.531

BLUMENSCHEIN provided lengthy explanations of his work to Gilcrease. Of *Moon, Morning Star, and Evening Star,* he wrote, "Very soon in the work I realized the big oval of the dancers must be the predominating figure. Then came the realization that I must sacrifice the two perpendicular 'Deer Mothers' as their perpendicular movement was too static. Then followed several months of painstaking execution of the details. This was a pleasurable part of the painting, but I had to be very careful to hold the details in place and maintain the rhythm. The 'Moon' 'Morning Star' and 'Evening Star' were added early in the work, as I felt the need of those

forms and lines to play against the big oval. . . . Many of the artists think [*Enchanted Forest*] is my best painting. It is a little finer in color perhaps, but there is virility in the 'Moon, Morning Star and Evening Star' that I believe will live a long time."

Of *Enchanted Forest,* Blumenschein wrote, "I combined the Deer Dance (this time including the Deer Mothers, as their perpendicular lines harmonized with the Aspens) and the beautiful background of aspens, and above Spruce and Pine, because it was a great setting for a primitive festival."

✛

ERNEST LEONARD BLUMENSCHEIN American, 1874-1960
MOON, MORNING STAR, AND EVENING STAR, 1922
Oil on canvas, 0137.2192
ENCHANTED FOREST, 1946
Oil on canvas, 0137.2191

HENNINGS came to the Southwest after study at the Royal Academy of Munich. A professional artist, he came to Taos not to escape the rigors of the traditional art capitals but to find new inspiration in the sun-filled landscape of the Southwest. He characterized his work as a combination of the fundamentals: draftsmanship design, form, rhythm, and color. This harmonious blend is seen in *Pueblo Indians,* a large

painting featuring women of Taos engaged in tasks of domestic simplicity. Painted late in Henning's career, this work is the product of careful planning and unhurried execution that contrasts dazzling light with strong shadows.

+

ERNEST MARTIN HENNINGS American, 1886-1957
PUEBLO INDIANS
Oil on canvas, 0137.2199

PHILLIPS, with J. H. Sharp, Ernest Blumenschein, Oscar Berninghaus, Irving Couse, and Herbert Dunton, founded the Taos Society of Artists, a group formed to promote the members' work. It was not a school, as the artists who were members were already trained professionals, and each retained his individuality. The artists found the landscape, people, and activities in the Taos Valley intriguing and novel subject matter, which they interpreted independently.

Phillips had a firm grounding and solid preparation in art. He had studied in America's finest schools and in Paris. His paintings, beautifully represented by *Corn Maidens,* are characterized by realism, particularly in his execution of human figures, combined with painterly brushwork in the landscape elements that serves to give movement and grace to his work.

+

BERT G. PHILLIPS American, 1868–1956
CORN MAIDENS
Oil on canvas, 0137.2197

One of Phillips's most unusual and compelling paintings, *Burial Procession – Penitente Ceremonial – Near Taos* relates one of the activities of Los Penitentes, a lay religious society in the Southwest. This brotherhood sometimes served as a burial society for its community, conducting the wake, funeral, and burial. Overt and covert religious symbols are revealed in the crosses carried by the mourners and the cruciform pattern of light that shines on the hills.

The composition, seen in both the study and finished painting, is also one of the most complex and modern created by Phillips. His exposure to Post-Impression during his study in Paris is reflected in the arrangement of the long line of anonymous figures, in the repeated pattern seen in the hillside, and in the primarily interest on flattened forms and abstract patterns.

+

BERT G. PHILLIPS American, 1868-1956
BURIAL PROCESSION (STUDY), 1946
Oil on canvas, 0137.513
BURIAL PROCESSION—PENITENTE CEREMONIAL—NEAR TAOS, 1946
Oil on canvas, 0137.2083

Too Old for the Rabbit Hunt illustrates one of Berninghaus's favorite themes, the contrast between generations. Painted when he was seventy-three years old, it is the last in a series of poignant works portraying a Taos Indian hunter forced by age to watch reflectively from the sidelines while younger riders enjoyed the thrill of the chase.

Berninghaus visited Taos, New Mexico, for the first time in 1899 and became a founding member of the Taos Society of Artists in 1912. Although he spent summers in Taos, until 1925 he maintained his home in St. Louis, Missouri, and was actively engaged in that city's art community. He also enjoyed a long association with the National Academy of Design, where he exhibited to acclaim for many years. He became an associate member of the Academy in 1926.

Berninghaus painted the everyday life of Taos Pueblo. Whether engaged in ceremonies or more mundane activities such as selling produce from an open-air stand, the Pueblo people captivated the artist. While most of the other members of the Taos Society of Artists had formal training in the fine arts, either in America, France or Germany, Berninghaus was trained as a commercial artist. When he turned his attention to fine arts, he pursued a singular style that encompassed intricate color patterns and designs. Not only the larger composition, but also the individual brushstroke was loaded with color and applied in short, succinct strokes. The effect was an almost sparkling surface.

+

OSCAR BERNINGHAUS American, 1874-1952
THE FRUIT VENDOR, 1946
Oil on canvas, 0137.519
TOO OLD FOR THE RABBIT HUNT, 1947
Oil on canvas, 0137.524

GROWING UP in the high plains of Texas, Hogue lived in what he called "the most luscious grassland in the world. . . an area which should never have been plowed." During the 1930s he witnessed the devastation of this grassland through extensive plowing and subsequent wind and water erosion, later remarking "I saw it all with my own dust-filled eyes. I considered it beautiful in a terrifying way." In reaction Hogue painted *Crucified Land*, part of a series of seven paintings that he called the Erosion Series that can be seen in opposition to the Regional painters who idealized the agrarian life.

As one of the few artists to deal with what was called the Dust Bowl, Hogue felt the subject deserved an original approach. In 1938 he defined a new technique he invented as "psycho-reality." In his approach, Hogue was "delving into mind reality by use of symbols arranged in a perfectly logical way, so that the observer feels he has actually experienced the scene."

+

ALEXANDRE HOGUE American, 1898-1994
CRUCIFIED LAND, 1939
Oil on canvas, 0127.2000

WILSON is a noted painter, lithographer, illustrator, muralist, teacher, and writer—an Oklahoma Renaissance man. Heir to the Regional painting style of Thomas Hart Benton and John Steuart Curry, Wilson focuses on the people and landscape of the Midwest. Much of his work revolves around the modern Indians of Oklahoma, exemplified by paintings such as *Shawnee Ribbon Bets*. The dynamic composition of vibrant, flowing ribbons reveals Wilson's superior draftsmanship and highly developed design sense. His Indian subjects are more than just colorful patterns, though; they are considered sensitive glimpses into community life.

Wilson organized the art department at Northeastern Oklahoma A&M and served as its director for fifteen years. Just before leaving to paint full-time in 1960, he secured his first major portrait commission. The directors of the newly formed Thomas Gilcrease Institute of American History and Art, commonly known as Gilcrease Museum, engaged him to paint its founder. Wilson recalls, "Tom Gilcrease knew the importance and was aware that I wanted very much to do a good job. I remember a remark he made to the members of the board of directors of the Institute—'I do not know if it will be a good painting when Wilson finishes it, but I do know it will be the best he can do. He's that kind of artist.' " The final result is indeed a good painting, showing Thomas Gilcrease seated outdoors in front of his original museum building, with the rolling Osage hills behind him.

The Native American Art Collection

KEVIN SMITH

Thomas Gilcrease sought to tell the story of America, with an emphasis on Native American cultures and the history of the West, through art. The museum founder's fundamental interest in Native America was due in part to his own Creek Indian ancestry. Evidence of his interest is dramatically illustrated by the vast amount of Native American art and artifacts he gathered. Collectors of Native American art objects often place a premium on them in accordance with their relative age. Gilcrease knew the value of that practice, yet he also knew the importance of collecting contemporary Native American art. He was patron to a number of Native American artists of his time and purchased over 500 paintings by 20th-century Native American artists alone. As a result, the museum not only tells the story of Native America through exhibition of objects thousands of years old, but also through modern paintings and sculptures.

Gilcrease, left, with Willard Stone and several of Stone's sculptures that were created for the Gilcrease collection.

Of the many Native American artists Gilcrease encouraged, three Oklahoma artists were to become close associates of the collector, painters Acee Blue Eagle (Creek/Pawnee), Woodrow (Woody) Crumbo (Creek/Potawatomi), and sculptor Willard Stone (Cherokee). Gilcrease employed all three in some capacity during the 1940s and their work helped to enrich the museum's collections greatly. In return, the patronage of a collector of Gilcrease's status helped to further the careers of each. All three are acknowledged to be among the most important Native American artists of the 20th century.

Artists like Crumbo, Stone, and Blue Eagle worked during the era that eminent artist and educator Ruthe Blalock Jones (Delaware/Shawnee/Peoria) has called the "golden age" of Indian painting in Oklahoma. Yet the Native American arts of painting and sculpture are ancient traditions. To fully appreciate modern expressions, it is important to understand that they reflect both change and continuity. It is helpful to focus especially on painting in order to understand the roles of evolution and tradition in modern native arts in general, as the medium of painting influenced the wider spectrum of modern native artistic expressions. In fact, the two sculptors featured in this section, Willard Stone and Allan Houser, both began their careers as painters before turning to sculpture. Like other 20th-century Native American artists, they found their careers to be inextricably connected with the history of Native American painting. Even as sculptors solely, both created art that reflected 20th-century concepts of Native American art that were first established through painting.

Painting traditions have existed throughout regions of North America for centuries. In the Southwest, painting for ceremonial and shamanistic purposes was practiced on small wooden figures and dance accoutrements, on the walls on rock cliffs, and on the interior walls of sacred kivas in the form of large-scale murals. On the Northwest Coast, massive two-dimensional images were painted to cover entire house fronts and ceremonial dance screens, and pigment was applied to sculptural works such as house posts and masks. On the Plains, painted compositions were applied to shields, teepees, clothing, containers, ceremonial objects, and war shields. And throughout various regions, the human body itself was a canvas for painted compositions that denoted prestige, political and religious status, for ceremonial purposes or to beautify. These and many other painting traditions were to undergo changes due to outlawing of tribal arts by non-Indian governments, replacement by trade items, missionary efforts to repress tribal traditions, exposure to European art, and the emergence of ethnic arts created exclusively for tourists and collectors.

Woody Crumbo, ca. 1949

The paintings featured here illustrate elements of cultural continuity in spite of such external pressures, but are not without evidence of non-Indian influences. Paintings by White Swan (Crow) and Carl Sweezy (Arapaho) illustrate individualized adaptation of Plains historic narrative traditions to fit the changes occurring at the end of the 19th century and the beginning of the 20th. Both were familiar with the historic Plains traditions of narrative painting, yet both clearly appropriated their own combinations of non-Indian materials, techniques, motivations or concepts in the execution of their works. Their paintings are representative of the acceptance of changing artistic traditions that would allow for the development of foundations of 20th-century Native American art.

By the 1930s, a newly established style of Native American painting prevailed, a style that only allowed individual adaptation or innovation within prescribed stylistic parameters. This school of painting is known variously as Flatstyle, Studio style, or traditional Indian painting. Flatstyle is most often characterized by the use of decorative color and line, an avoidance of European modeling and perspective, and a lack of emphasis on foreground and background. Most of the modern Native American paintings in the Gilcrease collection show the influence of this style. The development of Flatstyle painting occurred primarily in Oklahoma and New Mexico during the first half of the 20th century. In both states, important non-Indian patrons and institutions encouraged Native American artists to avoid European elements in their works such as point perspective, modeling of figures, and development of background or foreground. Instead, Indian artists were encouraged to create decorative "flat" compositions that featured some aspect of traditional Native American life. Thus, a simultaneous and parallel development of a new type of Indian painting occurred.

Bacone College, ca. 1942. At right, a detail from *Indian Gathering* by Stephen Mopope, in the Flatstyle.

In the Southwest, the most significant influence in establishing Flatstyle was the teacher Dorothy Dunn through her "Studio," established on the campus of the Santa Fe Indian School in 1932. While the works from the Studio conform to the same conventions as Flatstyle paintings from Oklahoma, they often show subtle differences common to the artists who studied together at the Studio. Thus, these works are often said to be in the Studio style. In Oklahoma, Oscar Jacobsen, director of the University of Oklahoma art department, encouraged a slightly different type of Flatstyle among Kiowa artists in the late 1920s and 1930s (see *Peyote Man* by Monroe Tsatoke). Other important institutional support for Flatstyle painting in Oklahoma came from Bacone College in Muskogee and the Philbrook and Gilcrease museums in Tulsa. Philbrook held the Annual National Exhibition of American Indian Painting from 1946 to 1979, providing the premier venue for promoting Native American painting to the world. Through its written rules for the "Indian Annual," Philbrook codified guidelines for Native American painting, allowing only the Flatstyle as the acceptable form for exhibition. Institutional preference for Flatstyle painting dominated much of the century and deeply impacted the field. However, important painters like Waldo Mootzka (Hopi), Dick West (Cheyenne), Oscar Howe (Yankton), and many others refused to remain within prescribed parameters. Apache artist Allan Houser began his career as a Flatstyle artist but eventually incorporated European methods of depicting three dimensions in his paintings. He ultimately moved to sculpture and became world renowned for his bronze and stone masterpieces. The debate over the validity of Flatstyle's exclusive claim became an important one in the 20th century, involving issues of Native American identity in general.

Since the time of Gilcrease's collecting of works by contemporary artists, many changes have taken place in Native American art. Artists have appropriated virtually every mainstream form of creative expression. The museum continues to promote and exhibit the works of contemporary Native American artists, just as the museum founder did during his lifetime. The exhibition of contemporary Native American art provides continuity of dedication to the perpetuation of Native American cultures through changing times. Yet, the paintings and sculptures of that "golden age" will always remain among the most valued treasures of Gilcrease. These works speak to the early modern challenges faced by Indian artists and bear witness to cultural endurance through adaptive artistic expression of aesthetic merit and historical significance.

Kiowa artists at the University of Oklahoma: Monroe Tsatoke, Stephen Mopope, Jack Hokeah, and Spencer Asah, in traditional dance attire.

THE CROW ARTIST WHITE SWAN achieved fame as both an artist and a warrior. Important painters Joseph Henry Sharp, Ernest T. Seton, and Charles Schreyvogel all painted his portrait. White Swan's fame was due, in part, to the fact that he was a scout for the cavalry at the Battle of the Little Bighorn. Thus, some of his paintings depict events from that famous battle. The three-tiered composition *War Record* presents an organized arrangement of separate vignettes, each representing a particular deed performed by White Swan during a battle. In the upper left and lower center scenes White Swan displays the pennant of the cavalry. He included the pennant in his paintings to indicate events that occurred at the Battle of the Little Bighorn. On the center tier, slightly to the left, the artist depicts himself spying on enemy Sioux through a telescope. To the right of that scene is a depiction

of White Swan attacking an enemy with a lance. The artist included some of the vignettes seen here in other paintings as he visually retold these stories throughout his life. However, the compositions of each event are altered to varying degrees from painting to painting. It may seem unusual that an artist depicting famous historic events should also be the subject of those paintings. Yet White Swan was simply following the common Plains Indian tradition of artistically recording important tribal events and personal exploits. *War Record* shows the transition from purely pictographic Plains painting to a more illusionistic style that would dominate Native American painting in the 20th century. The piece is consequently valuable as both a work of art and as an historical document.

+

WHITE SWAN Crow, c. 1851-1904
WAR RECORD
Watercolor, ink and pencil on muslin, 0226.589

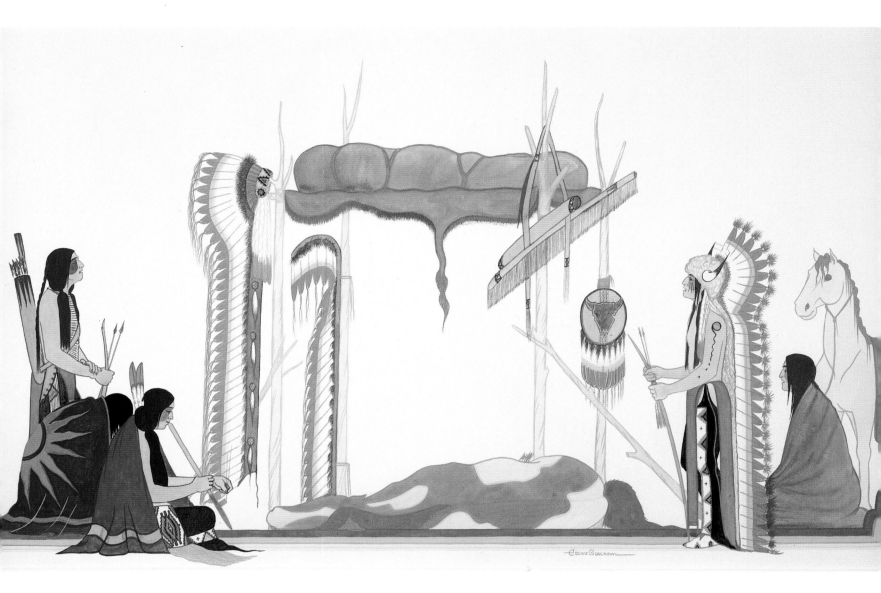

THE PAINTINGS of Archie Blackowl demonstrate the successful merging of the Studio style of Native American painting with the Kiowa and Bacone traditions from Oklahoma. Blackowl's most immediate influences were Woody Crumbo and Acee Blue Eagle, both of whom combined the Studio style of Santa Fe and the Kiowa style in their works. The results were erratic and the union was emergent and incomplete. With Blackowl's paintings, the blending of styles was further developed and refined. Blackowl, and other artists such as Blackbear Bosin, created the archetype Flatstyle painting that embodied the best of both traditions. Narrative drama and bold figural composition of the Oklahoma tradition are balanced with a mastery of the subtle use of design elements of the

Southwest tradition. This is not to say that the quality of Blackowl's paintings exceeds that of works by those who preceded him, only that his demonstrate a more mature stage in the evolution of Native American painting in Oklahoma. His best work stands not apart from, but alongside the other great Flatstyle painters of the past. Blackowl created strong paintings early in his career, having begun to paint seriously in the 1930s. Many of his paintings of the 1940s stand out because of their singular focus on authentic subjects within simple, but powerful, compositions. By the early 1950s, he began a period of experimentation, eventually arriving at a more complex style that he often used successfully in later paintings.

+

ARCHIE BLACKOWL Cheyenne, 1911-1992
BURIAL SCENE
Tempera on paper, 0227.378

PABLITA VELARDE'S ART IS BASED UPON EXPERIENCE. The ceremonies, family scenes, and landscapes of her works are reflections of what she actually witnessed. *Pueblo Craftsmen, Palace of the Governors* depicts an activity that continues in Santa Fe much as it did in 1941 when the painting was made. Pueblo artists still gather in the plaza to sell their creations displayed on blankets spread on the sidewalk. Early on, Velarde was among those Pueblo women artists chastised by some tribal traditionalists for painting. Even as a child in Dorothy Dunn's famous Studio School, she was treated harshly by the boys in her class. Velarde also broke with tradition by writing down her father's stories in an illustrated book, *Old Father Storyteller*. Santa Clara tradition held that writing down oral tradition could bring negative results. Velarde was confident in her actions, believing she was doing her part to preserve Santa Clara history in rapidly changing times. She was inspired by one of the earliest Pueblo painters, Tonita Peña, who introduced Velarde to painting. Velarde provided inspiration for future Native American women artists including her daughter, Helen Hardin.

+

PABLITA VELARDE Santa Clara, b. 1918
PUEBLO CRAFTSMEN, PALACE OF THE GOVERNORS
Watercolor on paper, 0227.565

At the time of Fred Kabotie's birth, the Hopi were divided into two factions defined by response to encroaching Anglo culture. One group was known as the "friendlies" and the other, the "hostiles." Kabotie's family belonged to the latter, suffering persecution for living a traditional life. Kabotie's father was once put in prison for opposing compulsory Anglo schooling of his children. Kabotie's art would later be dramatically impacted by his being raised during this time of struggle. Eventually, he was no longer able to avoid the agents of the government and was sent to Santa Fe Indian School in 1915. There he, like others, was forced to discard traditional language, religion, and traditions. This instilled a painful longing in Kabotie that would inspire him to focus on traditional Hopi life as subject matter for his

paintings. The opportunity to create such works came when John D. DeHuff was appointed superintendent of the Santa Fe Indian School. He and his wife, Elizabeth, played a major role in the career of Kabotie. Elizabeth DeHuff in particular encouraged Kabotie and other students to paint, arranging for them to substitute painting lessons at her home for other classes. Most remarkably, DeHuff encouraged her students to paint traditional tribal life, including ceremonials. This was against official government policy of the day, which was designed to eradicate Indian cultures through formal education. Kabotie became one of the most influential Native American painters of the Southwest. In 1937 he began a twenty-two-year teaching career at Hopi Pueblo, where he influenced many artists who looked to him for inspiration.

+

FRED KABOTIE Hopi, 1900-1986
PUEBLO GREEN CORN DANCE
Tempera on paper, 0137.1962

SOLOMON MCCOMBS was the cousin of Acee Blue Eagle, founder of the art department at Bacone College in Muskogee, Oklahoma. McCombs took lessons from his cousin there, along with other soon-to-be-famous Native American artists such as Dick West and Willard Stone. Typical of the Oklahoma school of Native American painting, McCombs's work is often narrative and dramatic. There is also a concern for creating a pleasing and balanced design. A painting such as *Preparation for the Ribbon Dance* might even be called decorative; however, the work actually contains an ethnographic veracity often lacking in Flatstyle paintings of the period. Rather than creating a nostalgic scene laced with Plains Indian imagery, a popular practice of the day, McCombs remains true to his Woodland heritage and even incorporates clothing made of commercially manufactured materials. Noted scholars and collectors have said that McCombs documented Creek lifestyle and worldview more thoroughly than did any other artist of his time. For McCombs, Native American Flatstyle painting was perfectly suited for the purpose of preserving Creek customs. His choice of Flatstyle was deliberate and significant as he considered it to be a truly indigenous style. He defended it against those who called it "Bambi art" and said it was a "true American art form." During his lifetime, McCombs did not receive the critical acclaim that some Indian artists, such as his cousin Acee Blue Eagle, enjoyed, yet his dedication to preserving Creek culture through illustrative paintings will be increasingly appreciated by future generations.

+

SOLOMON MCCOMBS Creek, 1913-1980
PREPARATION FOR THE RIBBON DANCE
Casein on paper, 0227.1674

In the 1920s and 30s a group of Kiowa artists in Oklahoma began a new movement in Native American art history. The group included Monroe Tsatoke, Stephen Mopope, Jack Hokeah, Lois Smokey, Spencer Asah, and James Auchiah. These Kiowas developed a unique painting style not seen before in Native American art. They did not use previously established Plains techniques of pictographic storytelling or visionary abstraction. Neither did they use European illusionistic devices such as modeling or point perspective. Under the tutelage of Oscar B. Jacobsen, director of the art department at the University of Oklahoma, the artists developed their unique type of painting known as the "Kiowa style." It became the foundation for the evolution of modern Native American painting in Oklahoma during the first half of the 20th

century. Kiowa painter Monroe Tsatoke had a clear vision for his art even at an early age. He sought to express the essence of the Kiowa worldview. He was demanding of himself in this endeavor, and if he felt a painting did not appropriately or adequately convey Kiowa culture, he would abandon it unfinished. Toward the end of his life, Tsatoke became increasingly concerned with depicting the Kiowa spiritual worldview, especially as experienced through the ceremonies and beliefs of the Native American Church. Paintings by Tsatoke and the other Kiowas of the movement provided the foundation for artists such as Woody Crumbo and Acee Blue Eagle. The artistic and cultural legacy of the Kiowa artists continues to inform and inspire Native American artists today.

+

MONROE TSATOKE Kiowa, 1904-1937
PEYOTE MAN
Tempera on paper, 0227.233

CARL SWEEZY was born on the Cheyenne-Arapaho Reservation when present-day Oklahoma was still Indian Territory. He learned to paint by the age of fourteen and by the turn of the century had become an important chronicler of ceremonial life. Hired by the anthropologists James Mooney and George Dorsey, Sweezy created works that provide important ethnographic information. He became a full-time painter after 1920, following his employment in other professions, including the Indian Police. Sweezy's most prolific period began when he was engaged by James Mooney. Yet even after his work for the anthropologist ended, he continued to paint enthusiastically until the end of his life. Sweezy essentially created his own style of painting, one that could be both informative and expressive. *Indian Religion* is a typical example of Sweezy's illustrative skill. Clearly shown are the participants of the ceremony, their clothing, and the ceremonial items that accompany the ceremonial activities. Sweezy sometimes worked in oil, unusual for an early 20th-century Native American artist as most worked exclusively in watercolor. His unique contributions are appreciated today by both anthropologists and art enthusiasts.

+

CARL SWEEZY Arapaho, 1879-1953
INDIAN RELIGION
Watercolor on paper, 0226.521

In 1946, Thomas Gilcrease offered Cherokee artist Willard Stone a position as artist-in-residence at the Gilcrease Museum and asked him to show through his art the "Indian's point of view of the 20th century." Stone created some of his most innovative and beautiful sculptures during his three-year tenure in this position, and Gilcrease and Willard Stone became friends as well as close associates. Occasionally, Stone even sought Gilcrease's advice and approval when developing a composition. Stone was receptive to his patron's request that he focus on contemporary themes. As a result, the artist created works dealing with topics such as modern warfare, nuclear weapons, and Christianity's influence on Native Americans. Because of the unique support he enjoyed, he was able to address topics not commonly approved of by Indian art enthusiasts of the time. In addition to considering contemporary topics, Stone also infused his works with modern style, drawing heavily from the Art Nouveau and Art Deco movements. *Tomorrow*, with its sweeping linear motif repeated in both exterior and interior contours, is a good example of the influence of the streamline Art Deco style. The Gilcrease collections also contain less stylized works by Stone. These sculptures were often inspired by nature and show little influence from any mainstream style. Stone was as adept at representing the natural flora and fauna of his environment as he was at representing the complex issues of modern times.

+

WILLARD STONE Cherokee, 1916-1985
TOMORROW
Wood, 1127.65

ALLAN HOUSER'S FATHER, SAMUEL HAOZOUS, was a runner for Geronimo and fought to keep the Apaches free in their homeland. As a child Houser listened as his elders spoke of tribal traditions and told family stories, and the rich history of his family and tribe became his deepest inspiration. He expressed his desire to portray Native American culture with dignity and integrity, and he remained true to this goal. Houser started as a painter. His first works are in the Flatstyle taught to Indian painters in Oklahoma and the Southwest in the first decades of the 20th century. However, his drawings and paintings became more and more three-dimensional as he experimented with depicting solid form.

He progressed to sculpture to satisfy his desire to express his artistic vision in three-dimensional space. Houser developed a stylized figurative expression that gained him worldwide acclaim. His personal style eventually became a recognizable standard in representing the native cultures of the Southwest. This aesthetic that distinguished his figurative works took forefront in the many abstract works he sculpted throughout his career. Houser received numerous honors, including a Guggenheim Scholarship in 1948, the Palmes d'Académiques in 1954, and the National Medal of Arts in 1992. *Sacred Rain Arrow* is displayed at the entrance to Gilcrease Museum.

+

ALLAN HOUSER Chiricahua Apache, 1915-1994
SACRED RAIN ARROW
Bronze, 0827.185

Woodrow Wilson ("Woody") Crumbo created dramatic compositions that feature fluid contours, unique linear dot patterns, and subtle expressiveness. *Blue Dancer* exhibits all of these characteristics. The piece also reveals Crumbo's reliance on the Kiowa style of depicting figures and clothing through its bright colors and use of strong contour lines. Crumbo was a friend and an advisor to Thomas Gilcrease, and he created some of his best works during the years of their close association. Consequently, the Gilcrease museum collections contain some of Crumbo's most significant works. Crumbo was well versed in Native American art and non-Indian art of the American West. Gilcrease often sought Crumbo's advice on acquiring significant works by both native and non-native artists for the museum's collections. Crumbo's enthusiasm for promoting contemporaries had a profound influence on the careers of

other Indian artists. As director of the Bacone College art department in Muskogee, Oklahoma, during the late 1930s he enthusiastically encouraged his students to promote their art. He also used his influence with important patrons such as Thomas Gilcrease to further the careers of students such as Willard Stone. He expressed pride in the growth of the Native American art movement of the 20th century and was a tireless promoter of Indian art, often appealing to curators and gallery directors on behalf of individual artists and the movement in general. Woody Crumbo is remembered not only for his artistic achievements but also for his influence on the careers of fellow artists and his role in the history of Gilcrease Museum. Crumbo's "peyote bird" design has been the distinctive logo of the museum from the time of Gilcrease to the present.

+

WOODY CRUMBO Potawatomi, 1912-1989
BLUE DANCER
Watercolor on paper, 0227.407

JEROME TIGER WAS UNUSUALLY GIFTED in his ability to observe and record with artistic precision. Essentially self-taught, Tiger possessed a command of draftsmanship that served as the foundation for his compositions. In 1962 he studied at the Cooper School of Art in Cleveland, Ohio, where he excelled in academic studio technique. Although this formal training was brief, it confirmed Tiger's artistic ability. For a time, Tiger painted in the Flatstyle that had evolved in the Southwest and Oklahoma as "traditional" Indian painting. Tiger used the style as a springboard for experimentation and growth. His delicate line, subtle composition, and soft palette were innovations that led to an entirely new look in Native American painting, often called the "Tiger style." It continues to be imitated by many Native

American artists. Tiger often imbued his works with emotion and a focus on the human condition in a manner not seen in Native American painting of the day. This aspect is visible in his many paintings of the forced removal of southeastern tribes to what is now Oklahoma. Tiger's effective treatment of universal human themes transcends the boundaries of genre or style. *The Four Moons* was created as a program cover for a ballet of the same name by Native American composer Louis Ballard. The ballet featured the four most renowned Indian ballerinas of Oklahoma—Yvonne Chouteau, Rosella Hightower, Moscelyne Larkin, and Marjorie Tallchief. *The Four Moons* was one of the last works painted by Jerome Tiger.

+

JEROME TIGER Creek/Seminole, 1941-1967
THE FOUR MOONS
Tempera and casein on paper, 0227.1673

Hopi artist Waldo Mootzka created paintings such as *Bean Dance* that are typical of the Southwest Watercolor Movement among Pueblo artists during the first half of the 20th century. Not typical of the period are Mootzka's fertility symbol paintings that employ very modern technique and subject matter. He is best known for these somewhat erotic compositions done in a style influenced by Art Deco. Though Mootzka was not formally trained, he learned by observing fellow artists such as the famous Hopi painter Fred Kabotie. Both artists rejected the Flatstyle taught to Indian artists of their day as the only legitimate form of Indian painting. This is evident by their measured use of European modeling to portray figures. During the 1930s Mootzka painted many depictions of various Kachinas and Pueblo ceremonies. Accurate detail, solid composition, and sensitive use of color characterize most of these works. Mootzka eventually progressed to create quite modern compositions and to focus on unusual subjects such as fertility rites and symbols. Such paintings show the influence of Art Deco, a movement that affected Indian painting and other traditional tribal arts, including ceramics, during the early 20th century. Even in his more conservative works, Mootzka was somewhat experimental in the use of line and texture. He was, perhaps unconsciously, paving the way for innovation by future artists. Indeed, his contemporaries commented that he was ahead of his time. Art historians too have credited Mootzka with being a vital transitional figure in the history of Hopi painting.

+

WALDO MOOTZKA Hopi, 1910-1940
BEAN DANCE
Tempera on paper, 0237.196

Acee Blue Eagle was born in 1907 on the Wichita Indian Reservation near Anadarko, Oklahoma. He attended government Indian schools and graduated from the University of Oklahoma. He studied under Oscar B. Jacobson, founder of the university's art department and patron of the Kiowa painters who established the stylistic foundation for Oklahoma Native American Flatstyle painting. Blue Eagle knew the Kiowa artists and his early works were heavily influenced by their art. He later developed his own style, partly by incorporating influences from the Pueblo painters of the Southwest. Acee Blue Eagle did much to popularize 20th-century Native American painting. He traveled extensively throughout the United States presenting lectures on Native American art and performing Native American dance and music for schools and social organizations. In 1935, he lectured on Native American art at Oxford University, England. That same year, he became the founding director of the art department at Bacone College in Muskogee, Oklahoma. The school would become a center for the development of Native American painting in Oklahoma. In the 1940s, Blue Eagle became a personal friend of Thomas Gilcrease and created a number of works for the Gilcrease collections. His paintings often featured such subjects as buffalo hunts, Plains Indian ceremonies, and genre scenes of southeastern tribal life. While some of Blue Eagle's works present almost stereotypical depictions of Plains Indians, others, like *Medicine For Children*, are relatively accurate portrayals of the cultures of Southeastern tribes. Blue Eagle continued painting until his death in 1959. Memorial services for the artist were held at Gilcrease Museum.

+

ACEE BLUE EAGLE Creek/Pawnee, 1907-1959
MEDICINE FOR CHILDREN
Watercolor on paper, 0227.457

Harrison Begay entered the Santa Fe Indian School in 1934 where he studied under Dorothy Dunn. His work exemplifies the Studio style taught by Dunn. Compositions have little or no background, no point perspective or modeling, and feature solid areas of color contained within contour lines. This Flatstyle painting developed concurrent with the Flatstyle painting tradition in Oklahoma at the University of Oklahoma and Bacone College. Begay's subject matter and palette varied. When painting ceremonial scenes, he used bolder colors and more active figures, often against an empty background. In contrast, delicate lines, pastel colors, and peaceful settings characterize Begay's series of Navajo women spinning and weaving. There is also some, if minimal, attention to the background. Foliage in particular is used to frame the composition and to imply a natural and pleasant outdoor setting. The paintings are pleasing and highly decorative, yet they also contain accurate and interesting information about Navajo life. Begay studied the material culture of Navajo tribal ceremonies and daily life to provide a foundation for his art. He was particularly interested in gathering images from Navajo weavings and drypaintings. His interest in accurately depicting his tribal culture combined with his sense of pleasing design and composition led to many awards for his paintings. In 1954 he was awarded the French Palmes d' Academiques. His works are still considered some of the finest examples of Native American painting of the Southwest.

+

HARRISON BEGAY Navajo, born 1917
NAVAJO WOMAN SPINNING
Tempera on paper, 0237.160

JULIAN MARTINEZ is best known for his role in supporting the work of his famous wife, potter Maria Martinez. Maria gathered the clay, formed the vessel, and oversaw firing while Julian composed and painted the two-dimensional compositions that would create the black-on-black surface of the ceramics. It was a common Pueblo tradition for husband and wife to collaborate on the production of ceramics, and such collaborations resulted in some of the finest ceramics from the Southwest.

Part of the success of Maria's pottery was due to Julian's exuberant designs, which he researched and kept in a notebook that he added to over time. By the 1920s he had visited public museums and other pueblos and filled his sketchbooks with prehistoric, historic, and contemporary designs providing the foundation for the invention of his own compositions. His painting activities also included works on

paper such as *Pottery Design* and murals in public institutions in the Southwest. Although he used traditional culture as a foundation, Martinez was influenced by Anglo art in his use of line. He often simplified Pueblo designs to create elegant Native American Art Deco expressions.

After World War I, Santa Fe patrons encouraged self-taught Pueblo artists, many of whom were from San Ildefonso Pueblo. Martinez was among these artists, most of whom began experimenting with somewhat illusionist or narrative works. As was common at the time, patrons discouraged such attempts and advised artists to paint traditional Pueblo designs that were more abstract and decorative.

+

JULIAN MARTINEZ San Ildefonso, 1897-1943
POTTERY DESIGN
Ink and watercolor on paper, 0236.257

POP CHALEE's experiences with art began during childhood in Taos, New Mexico, where she often visited the studios of the Taos Colony artists. Later, she studied painting in Dorothy Dunn's Studio classes at the Santa Fe Indian School. Upon her graduation, she took Dunn's advice and opened a studio in Santa Fe. She began painting professionally full time in 1936 at the age of thirty.

Pop Chalee painted several forest scenes during her career. Although they vary, each features the artist's signature style. Pop Chalee noted that the Taos Mountains were the inspiration for her whimsical forest scenes. Trees, plants and animals are indicated by delicate contour lines. Foliage is represented in a spare, symbolic manner. The very simple representation of some of the animals in her art is her own invention as much are as the imaginative compositions themselves. In some instances, her animals are inspired by those painted on traditional Southwest ceramics.

The artist was of European, East Indian, and American Indian ancestry and was conscious of her mixed heritage. She made aesthetic comparisons between the cultures, for example saying the Apache Crown Dance appeared "quite Oriental" to her. She observed that ancient Egyptians created art that reflected their natural environment, and she felt that Native American Flatstyle watercolor paintings were similar in form and meaning. Many Native American paintings from the Southwest feature depictions of ceremonies, individual figures, or traditional ceramic designs. Although she also painted such images, Pop Chalee is best known for her more imaginative and original works such as *Forest Scene*.

+

POP CHALEE Taos, 1906-1993
FOREST SCENE
Tempera on paper, 0237.527

116

STEPHEN MOPOPE was a descendant of noted Kiowa warriors and artists. Distinguished members of his family included Silverhorn (Haungooah) and Hakok. These two men taught young Mopope how to paint on hides in the old Kiowa way. In the 1920s Mopope made the somewhat abrupt change from the more traditional hide painting to modern easel painting. In addition to painting, Mopope learned Kiowa religious and social traditions from his family. He was an active traditional dancer and singer and sponsored dances on his farm in southwestern Oklahoma. These experiences informed his art throughout his career. The culture pictured in his paintings was witnessed through personal experience. His lifelong participation in ceremonies makes his artwork more authentic than that of many later artists who participated in fewer traditions. Nevertheless, works such as *Indian Gathering* do contain an element of nostalgia.

Although Kiowa traditional gatherings continued during his lifetime, *Indian Gathering* is an image of a fondly remembered past, albeit a not too distant one. In the late 1920s, Mopope was among a group of Kiowa artists who studied painting at the University of Oklahoma. Under the tutelage of Oscar B. Jacobsen, director of the art department, the artists developed a unique type of painting known as the "Kiowa style." It became the foundation for Native American painting in Oklahoma during the first half of the 20th century. *Indian Gathering* demonstrates the Kiowa style as well as Mopope's ability to work on a large scale. The work contains more expressive attention to background than do most Kiowa paintings of the period. Yet, even when expressive, Mopope's paintings are controlled, understated, and carefully composed.

+

STEPHEN MOPOPE Kiowa, 1898–1974
INDIAN GATHERING
Oil on canvas, 0217.2013

RUTHE BLALOCK JONES is the most prominent Native American artist effectively continuing the Flatstyle painting tradition. Internationally exhibited and often a top winner at the Santa Fe Indian Art Market, Jones uses various styles of painting and printmaking in addition to working in the Flatstyle tradition. Although she earnestly pursues experimentation, especially in acrylics, her constant dedication to Flatstyle painting has resulted in a refinement and advancement of the style. *Medicine Woman* provides one example that illustrates her sophisticated development of what once was considered a simple and decorative type of painting. Although Native American Flatstyle painting does not employ European techniques to create illusion, the piece is nevertheless remarkably convincing. At least part of that result can be attributed to the artist's dedication to knowing the subject and to having an authentic understanding of it through personal experience and participation. Such familiarity results in the inclusion of realistic compositions and details. Through her Medicine Women series, Jones expresses her great respect for the members and ceremonies of the Native American Church. Jones began participating in the ceremonies herself at an early age, witnessing firsthand the subject matter of the Medicine Women paintings. Jones is also a master of technique, incorporating careful, expert drawing and complex color combinations in her work. The level of artistic skill necessary to create paintings such as *Medicine Woman* was rarely demonstrated by previous Flatstyle artists. No other artist has advanced the style so significantly while maintaining its integrity within the context of "traditional" rules of execution.

+

RUTHE BLALOCK JONES Delaware/Shawnee/Peoria, born 1939
MEDICINE WOMAN
Gouache on mat board, 0227.1942

NORMAN AKERS is known primarily for his work in oil on large canvases. He attended the Institute of American Indian Arts in Santa Fe from 1982 to 1984. In 1988 he moved to Champaign-Urbana, Illinois, to pursue an MFA in painting. There, he began creating his very personal "dreamscapes." In these works he attempts to make sense of the daily schisms between the old and the new, between Osage and Western worldviews, and between personal and cultural experiences. The paintings are expressionistic and contain a mingling of the abstract, the figurative and the surreal. *Collision of Heavenly Structures* illustrates the surrealistic aspect of Akers's works by presenting recognizable objects in unusual relationships to one another. His works are autobiographical. He developed his personal "symbology" while a student in Illinois to help him to deal with the growing disconnection

he was feeling from the people, environment, and personal experiences that were a part of his life in Oklahoma. The autobiographical characteristics of his paintings are the obvious and inevitable results of that process. Personal images appear in chaotic, yet choreographed, compositions reflecting his need to connect with family, environment, and with traditional tribal beliefs. These images are the icons that make up his "symbology." The icons often allude to cultural traditions. The lunch box that appears in this and other works refers to an Osage funeral custom. While some symbols refer to tribal traditions, others refer to entirely personal experiences. The creative exploration of the subconscious provides the vital foundation for surrealist artists. For Akers, it also provides a way to discover personal identity and worldview.

+

NORMAN AKERS Osage/Pawnee, born 1958
COLLISION OF HEAVENLY STRUCTURES
Oil on canvas, 0127.2486

BOBBY MARTIN initially worked outside Native American art circles while earning degrees in painting and printmaking because he felt no affinity with popular subjects or styles of Native American art. He consciously resisted any pan-Indian themes in his work, regardless of their popularity. Martin focused first on researching his family history and second on expressing his discoveries through a personal style. He felt this process was more honest than imposing Native American art trends upon his identity. Martin's interest in his Muscogee ancestry focused primarily on family experiences in the late 19th and early 20th centuries. Martin's work is significant in part because he successfully explores this part of Native American history overlooked by other artists. His research revealed a family history rooted in the Christian mission experience in Indian Territory, and later, Oklahoma. He studied mission postcards, memorabilia and family photos. Martin recreates images from these various sources using acrylic paint on canvas. This universal and nostalgic image type, seen on a large scale, engages the viewer's attention as if journeying through an album of old photos. The use of sepia colors produces an "old photo" effect, and preserves the warmth and intimacy of a family portrait. Martin presents Native American people in settings rarely seen in Native American art. There is poignancy in these paintings. Renderings of family members and tribal ancestors are juxtaposed with the impersonal icons of assimilation. The result is a remade family photo album haunted by the history of change for Indian people.

+

BOBBY C. MARTIN Creek, born 1957
APR '55
Mixed media on canvas, 0127.2503

The Anthropology Collection

DANIEL C. SWAN

The Anthropology Department of Gilcrease Museum curates an expansive and diverse array of materials. Numbering approximately 300,000 individual pieces, the collections include archaeological, historic, and contemporary objects produced by the indigenous populations of the Western Hemisphere. This material encompasses utilitarian, ceremonial, and aesthetic objects spanning from Clovis spear points that date to 15,000 years ago to contemporary works of Native American traditional arts. The combined anthropological collections of the museum provide a resource for scholarly research and publication, interpretive exhibitions, student education programs, and collaborations with Native American communities and their members.

Thomas Gilcrease with an artifact display in the late 1950s.

Thomas Gilcrease, left, with Nelson Glueck, center, and Alfred Aaronson in the late 1950s. Dr. Glueck was an internationally prominent archaeologist and scholar. Aaronson was one of the civic leaders who helped keep the Gilcrease collections in Tulsa. The basket Glueck holds is of central California origin.

Thomas Gilcrease employed a number of methods to create the core anthropological collections of the museum. These included purchase of individual objects, acquisition of complete collections assembled by others, and assembly of collections through systematic research. Clear examples for each type of collecting activity can be isolated in the anthropological materials of the museum.

In the late 1940s Gilcrease began to add anthropological objects to his growing collections of fine art a few selected pieces at a time. In the late 1940s and early 1950s he turned to the same strategy he had employed in building the fine art collections of the museum, purchasing private collections of significant scale and quality. The purchase of the Lloyd Bolles collection of southwestern ceramics from the Mesa Verde region in 1948, the Emil Lenders collection of ethnographic materials in 1950, and the Harry J. Lemley collection of archaeological artifacts in 1955 brought immediate depth and scale to the anthropology collections of the Gilcrease Museum. The Lenders and Lemley collections are well documented and provide a core resource for both museum research and exhibitions. Lenders was a German born and trained artist who achieved acclaim for his wildlife and western genre paintings. Settling in Oklahoma, he became an active dealer and collector of Native American traditional arts. Harry Lemley, a judge from Fayetteville, Arkansas, had dedicated much of his life and considerable resources to building one of the most important private collections of pottery and other materials from the mound building cultures of Arkansas, Oklahoma, and the surrounding region.

Following the original transfer of his collection to the City of Tulsa in 1955, Gilcrease continued to collect fine art and manuscript materials although this activity was eclipsed by his growing interest in archaeology. The subsequent addition of other private collections in the late 1950s and early 1960s added geographic and temporal scope to the anthropology holdings of the museum. Important collections purchased during this period by the Gilcrease Foundation include those of Madge Hardin Walters (Northern Plains Indian materials), T. Hugh Young (Archaic and Mississippian lithics, ceramics, and ground stone), and the Gibson collection (Hopewell and Spiro Mound vessels, effigy pipes, and statues). Gilcrease quickly realized the value of systematic field excavations as a source of well documented museum specimens. His growing passion for field archaeology is well evidenced through his sponsorship of numerous field excavations in the period of 1955/62, in many of which he was an active participant. Excavation of sites in Arkansas, Missouri, Illinois, Tennessee, and Mississippi produced important assemblages of objects created by the members of the Hopewell and Mississippian civilizations of North America.

The anthropology collections at Gilcrease have continued to grow since the death of our founding patron. Through his bequest, the Gilcrease Foundation donated the collections he had acquired between 1955 and 1962. The addition of these extensive archaeological materials to the permanent collection established the national reputation of the Anthropology Department of Gilcrease Museum. The Thomas Gilcrease Museum Association continued this tradition through the purchase, in 1982, of the Frank Soday collection of archaeological materials.

Donation has long been an important source of collection growth. The first known gift of a private collection to Gilcrease Museum was the 1939 donation of 4,600 archaeological objects from Delaware County, Oklahoma, by Albert Reed. In the 1970s Dr. David Harner made extensive gifts to the museum that included collections of historic Mexican masks, pre-Columbian ceramics, and Mississippian artifacts from Arkansas. Numerous others have donated single pieces that have particularly enhanced the museum's collection of Navajo textiles and southwestern baskets and ceramics. The anthropology collections of the museum have benefited from the recent gifts of personal collections by Native American donors. I believe that Thomas Gilcrease would take great pride in the decisions of these individuals to select Gilcrease Museum as the repository for their family collections, and, even more importantly, the information and stories that surround their creation, use, and cultural significance.

Gilcrease at an archaeological dig in the late 1950s.

The ethnographic collection of the museum has also grown through a number of initiatives supported by the Thomas Gilcrease Museum Association. The *Las Artes de Mexico, Euchee Custom Ways,* and *Symbols of Faith and Belief* exhibitions included systematic acquisitions of contemporary works in the traditional arts to better interpret the aesthetic and cultural significance of the archaeological and historical objects in the collection.

The anthropology collection of Gilcrease Museum has received international attention for its quality and breadth. In the disciplines of archaeology and ethnology the collection is one of the most important in a public institution. Our mission to provide the highest standard of collections stewardship, to facilitate enhanced public access, and to continue a tradition of collaboration with Native American communities will insure that these materials are available to broad audiences into the future.

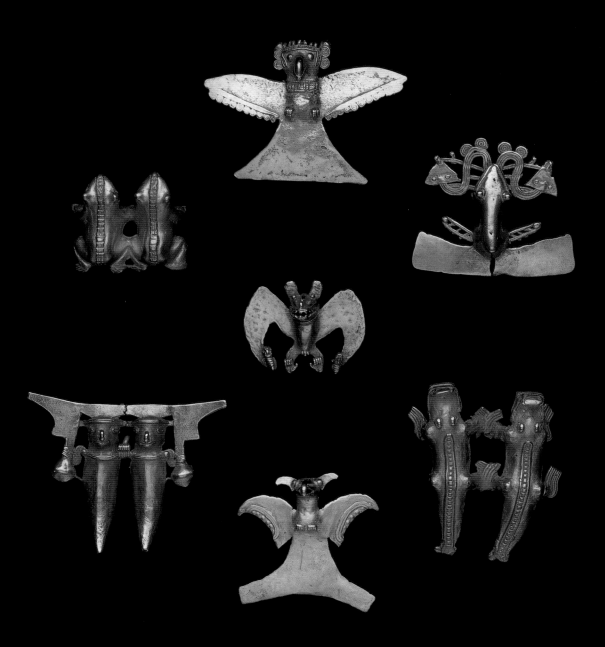

THE INDIGENOUS PEOPLE OF SOUTH AND CENTRAL AMERICA created ritual instruments and objects for personal adornment in silver, gold, copper, platinum, and tin. The people of western Panama and of adjacent areas in Costa Rica lived in a region rich in mineral resources. The widespread wearing of gold pendants in the form of eagles was noted in the journal of Columbus when he opened the region to conquest in 1502.

Craftsman from the Chiriqui, Cocle, Veragua, and other indigenous groups in the region excelled in their gold artistry, employing refined methods of casting, soldering, and brazing to create highly detailed figures and abstract forms. Their metallurgical knowledge included the discovery that the melting point of gold could be greatly reduced when it was mixed with copper to create an alloy referred to as tumbaga.

The color shift produced by this admixture is evident in many of the pieces in the Gilcrease collection. The Indian people of this region also employed various techniques to expose a layer of high quality gold on the surface of objects cast from tumbaga. Eagles, frogs, sea horses, and crocodiles are common designs in gold work from Panama. These and other natural figures are powerful symbols in the cosmologies of the indigenous people of Mesoamerica. Spanish Colonial officials destroyed most of these indigenous artworks, melting them into ingots for more efficient shipment to Spain.

PANAMANIAN AND COSTA RICAN GOLD ORNAMENTS, CA. 1000–1500 CE (CURRENT ERA)
Panama and Costa Rica
(l-r) top 56.37; second row 56.217, 226, 207; bottom 56.216, 157, 156

Native Americans have a long tradition of using art to record the real and mythical events that are important in the histories of a people. Long before European exchange, the indigenous people of North America used stone, shell, ivory, bone, hide, bark, and other materials as canvases for designs rendered in diverse media and techniques.

In the Great Plains region this was the artwork of men, who painted on hides used to construct teepees and their linings, clothing items, and objects important to warfare and religion.

These paintings were composed of a series of unrelated vignettes that portrayed various events, activities and scenes. Among certain communities, paintings on hides served as "winter counts" that recorded the history of a local community through the public selection of a single event from the previous year to be rendered in pictographic fashion on the hide. These "counts" were important aids in the telling of the oral history of a local group or band.

Embellished robes of elk and bison form one of the central painting traditions of the historic period. The robes were public statements of autobiographical events and accomplishments. A lexicon of symbols that developed over time could convey geographic place, tribal affinity, and personal identification. A special iconography was employed to represent the passage of time and physical motion. This bison robe includes a large number of painted vignettes that present a Sundance pole and associated dancers, courting scenes, episodes of intertribal warfare, buffalo hunts, scenes of women wearing cradleboards, and the use of dog and horse travois.

+

LAKOTA PAINTED BUFFALO HIDE, LATE 19TH CENTURY
Northern Plains
Emil Lenders Collection, 89.49

Bags with shoulder straps were indispensable among the native peoples of eastern North America. Early examples were constructed from hide and decorated with vegetal dyes and porcupine quill or moose hair embroidery. Indian people from the Great Lakes region also used a range of vegetable fibers to produce plaited, twined, and woven utility bags. Each of these traditional art forms contributed to the design and decorative detail of Ojibwe shoulder bags of the 19th and 20th centuries.

The fur trade of the 18th century provided ready access to European glass beads, thread, needles, and fabrics. The Indian people of the Great Lakes region developed a variety of ingenious techniques to produce woven beadwork, using a supporting base of warp thread and attaching the beads with the weft. Woven beadwork can be produced through the use of various types of looms, ranging from a fixed pole and a bow to a closed wooden frame. At its most sophisticated, a wooden heddle was used to weave double warp threads to set the beads.

Throughout the 19th century, Ojibwe shoulder bags increased in size and decorative detail, while their utilitarian function diminished to the point where they were no longer bags at all, but important accessories to the ceremonial wear of men. This bag incorporates a number of design characteristics common in early Ojibwe woven beadwork, including the arrangement of the central design element in an "X" pattern, two different designs for the beadwork on the front and back of the strap, and the eight-pointed star and pinwheel motifs. The small section of open appliqué work at the top of the panel was one of the first seed bead techniques known among the Ojibwe, gained through exposure to Iroquois, Huron, and Ottawa designs and techniques.

+

OJIBWE SHOULDER BAG, CA. 1870
Western Lake Superior Region
84.1724

The Huichol Indians live in small, scattered settlements in the rugged Sierra Madre region of western Mexico. Weaving, embroidery, beadwork, and yarn painting are physical manifestations of the religious devotion of the Huichol people. In the context of Huichol life these artistic works are best viewed as prayers, meant to insure the health, fertility, and prosperity of individuals and of the community as a whole. Huichol religious beliefs encourage men and women to pursue spiritual completion through their artwork. Artists may seek divine guidance and power for their art, and a master of weaving, embroidery, and beadwork, like the shaman, is a guardian of knowledge to be passed along to future generations.

Early Huichol yarn paintings depicted authentic, but haphazard, arrangements of sacred and decorative symbols. "Storytelling" works were developed more recently, often at the suggestion of anthropologists. Yarn paintings are made by applying an even coat of beeswax mixed with resin to one side of a board, scratching a design into the wax, and then laying in the figures and other details with strands of colored yarn.

This painting incorporates a range of religious symbolism drawn from both traditional Huichol belief and Christianity, to which the Huichol have been missionized repeatedly over the past five centuries. Executed in fine embroidery floss, this yarn painting is among the most detailed and complex of modern examples. The piece was acquired by Gilcrease Museum from the prestigious Museo de Artes Populares y Industriales in Mexico City, Mexico.

+

HUICHOL YARN PAINTING, 1993
Nayarit, Mexico
99.190

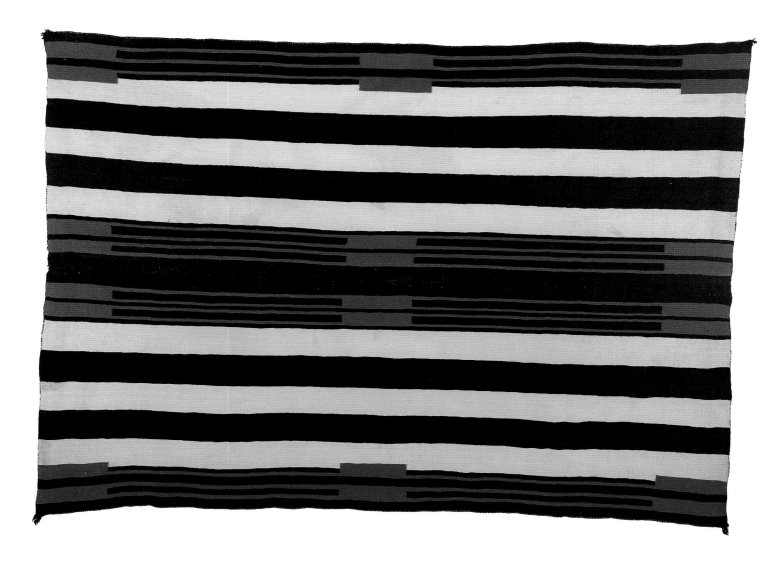

Perhaps no single indigenous art is more uniquely identified with a tribal community than is weaving with the Navajo. Following their migration to the Southwest in the late 15th century, ancestral Navajo people adopted many economic patterns from the original Puebloan inhabitants of the area. Among their important adaptations was the weaving of fabric on an upright loom. Today, this tradition is best known from the varied design rugs that are central to contemporary Navajo art and commerce.

This second phase Chief Blanket was produced at a time when the Navajo people were renowned for the blankets they wove from homespun wool. In the 1820s, the Navajo began to trade their blankets to neighboring tribes and within a relatively short period found markets among Native American and colonial communities in the United States and Mexico. The name "Chief Blanket" is somewhat of a misnomer, deriving from the fact that only political leaders of the time could afford to trade for Navajo textiles.

Woven from handspun wool in both natural and dyed colors, this blanket exhibits the classic design scheme of the mid 19th century, where groups of six red blocks are used to interrupt the indigo blue bands at the center and edges of earlier First Phase blankets. Suitable red dye was difficult to obtain in the Navajo region during this period. Here the red is obtained from bayeta, a wool trade cloth that was dyed red with cochineal, the powdered bodies of cactus beetles from Mexico. Navajo weavers raveled the cloth and then spun the fibers back into yarn. To match the smaller size of bayeta yarn, Navajo weavers reduced the size of their traditional homespun yarn. This development greatly enhanced the fine weave found in many Classic Period Navajo textiles.

+

NAVAJO SECOND PHASE BLANKET, CA. 1860

Arizona

97.26

FEATHER FANS are one of the most important objects associated with the Native American Church, evocative of the complex bird symbolism associated with the religion. In addition to the leader's fan that accompanies the ritual staff in its "rounds" throughout the ceremony, many participants possess and use individual feather fans. Bird symbolism in the religion focuses on the role of birds as messengers carrying prayers to the Creator. Feathers and fans similarly transfer the blessings of cedar smoke, the fire, and sacred objects to participants as they touch feathers to these holy elements and then pat their bodies.

This fan is a "loose" form, where the feathers are attached to the handle by thin leather strips that allow them to float free, in contrast to the rigid feather settings of "flat" fans. This fan incorporates the feathers of diverse species of birds, including scissortail, macaw, and other parrots. Feathers in

loose fans are often trimmed to uniform size and varied shapes and are further embellished through the addition of brightly colored trim feathers, wrapped thread, and beadwork. Twisted leather fringe made of finely cut buckskin is adorned with sterling silver bands with crosses and a heart attached as decorative dangles. Handles of fans are decorated with glass seed beads attached one at a time through a beading technique referred to as "gourd stitch." Design patterns often incorporate abrupt color juxtaposition, filled parallelograms, and symbols drawn from the ceremonial setting and ritual ceremony of the religion. Artistic patterns established through the artwork inspired by the Native American Church have greatly influenced trends and directions for many traditional Native American arts in Oklahoma and throughout the United States.

+

KIOWA FEATHER FAN, CA. 1940
Oklahoma
84.218

THE ANCIENT OLMEC people of modern-day Veracruz provided an important foundation for the Maya and Aztec civilizations of the first millennium. Known for their monumental sculpture, pyramids, and temples, the Olmec also developed the first hieroglyphic writing system in the Americas and made pioneering advances in the fields of astronomy and calendrics. Among their aesthetic accomplishments were figural sculptures made of hollow ceramic. The ability to create hollow figures without the use of an interior support armature requires great knowledge and skill. Slips of gray, white, and red lend subtle colors to the highly polished surfaces of these works.

These figurines often take a form referred to as "Olmec babies." While some do in fact represent babies, others are quite ambiguous as to age and gender. Some assume highly stylized representation of humans with elongated heads and distorted proportion of body and limb. The symbolism of these figures remains speculative and a source of debate among modern archaeologists. Interpretations include the representation of physical deformities, a transformation state for shamans and other religious specialists, and a were-jaguar. The latter is evidenced on this figure by the thin, cat-like shape of the eyes. This Olmec figurine is considered to be among the best extant examples of this art form.

+

OLMEC HUMAN FIGURE, CA. 1,000 BCE – 400 CE
Tlatilco, Mexico

54-7749

THE ADVENT OF CLIMATIC PATTERNS more conducive to agriculture and the emergence of a more productive variety of maize in the 8th century supported the greatest urban development among the indigenous people of North America. By 950, Cahokia, located near the current city of St. Louis, was the largest urban area north of Mexico with at least 10,000 inhabitants. At the height of growth and distribution, Mississippian towns were located from Wisconsin south to Oklahoma and east to Georgia and Alabama.

The cities, towns, and farming communities of the Mississippian world were united through their participation in the Southeastern Ceremonial Complex. The religious and political hierarchy produced a system of rank and power that gained tangible expression through a variety of artistic enterprises. Copper ear spools, shell gorgets, polished stone celts, and finely decorated ceramics were embellished with designs symbolic of Mississippian cosmology and worldview.

This graceful double bottle of thin black ware is engraved with delicate crosshatching separated by areas of highly polished surface to create a serpentine design on the stirrup portion of the vessel. Some of the red pigment that was rubbed into the engraving to accentuate the pattern remains visible. The thin-walled construction found in this ceramic tradition is evidence of the high quality local clays dug from the stream and riverbanks in west-central Arkansas and the innovation of a burnt shell temper to strengthen the fired vessel.

+

MISSISSIPPIAN CERAMIC BOTTLE, 400 – 1100 CE
Yell County, Arkansas

54.1523

IN THE LAST DECADES OF THE 19TH CENTURY, collectors representing the great American museums of the day overwhelmed the Indian people of the American Southwest in their quest for "ancient" ceramic wares. As both the supply of these precious heirlooms and the willingness to trade them away declined, Hopi women began to reproduce these pots to meet the demand. Among these enterprising women was Nampeyo, born in the village of Hano at the northwest tip of First Mesa, on the current Hopi Indian Reservation in Arizona. Nampeyo was well suited to this task based on her longstanding interest in the design elements found on potshards from the prehistoric sites she encountered in her travel of the mesa and the surrounding areas. She was particularly inspired by the abstract bird designs found in the shards of polychrome vessels from the ruins of Sikyatki, an abandoned village on the mesa. Nampeyo expanded this research as archaeologists began to excavate sites in the Hopi region. As "scientific" and popular

attention waned, most Hopi women returned to the production of ceramic vessels for the use of their families, embellishing them with traditional designs and schemes. Nampeyo continued to focus on the abstract, free-flowing design elements that she employed and refined over the course of her career.

This jar is decorated with two sets of alternating designs used with great frequency by Nampeyo between 1912 and 1915. The design featured here is an abstract bird motif that uses feather "fans" to represent wings and tail, with the elongated beak appearing to tuck under the wing. It is flanked by a highly stylized Kachina design. This jar was obtained by the museum as a piece in the William R. Leigh studio collection. Leigh painted several portraits of Nampeyo and her family members, including one in the Gilcrease collection of Nampeyo's oldest daughter, Annie, who carried on the Hano Polychrome tradition.

+

NAMPEYO Hopi, ca. 1860-1942
POLYCHROME JAR, CA. 1925

54-4396

"MOCCASIN," the Anglicized version of the French interpretation of an Algonkian Indian word, has become the generic term for Native American footwear in North America. Constructed from the tanned hide of bison, deer, moose, caribou, and antelope, moccasins and boots assumed divergent forms throughout the continent. Moccasins created from a single piece of hide, cut and sewn according to intricate patterns, produced the "soft sole" types that dominated in the eastern Woodlands and Great Lakes regions. In the Plains and Southwest areas, moccasins and boots commonly employed hard soles of untanned rawhide to provide greater protection and longer wear.

Considerable effort was invested in the design nuances and decorative embellishment of Native American footwear,

bringing aesthetic elements and symbolic meanings to an otherwise utilitarian object. Adorned with embroidered porcupine and bird quills, ribbon work, paint, and beadwork, moccasins provided challenging arenas for artistic expression. Many groups developed separate styles and decorative elements for footwear depending on the age and gender of the wearer. The interpretation of design motifs includes realistic elements of the physical world, abstract symbolism from the cosmos, and representations of supernatural forces. It is interesting to note that moccasin design and decoration, particularly for women, provided one of the most tenacious elements of tribal distinctiveness into the 20th century.

+

MOCCASINS, LATE 19TH AND EARLY 20TH CENTURIES

North America

(l-r) top 84.273, 333, 388, 409,; second row 84.381, 292, 383, 331

third row 84.285, 308,339, 356; fourth row 84.320, 319, 322, 415, 310

Hopewell cultural complex is the name given by archaeologists to the cultures of the Middle Woodland period in Illinois. Hopewell local organization consisted of relatively small family-based communities that were located on river terraces adjacent to their fields. The Hopewell period is significant for the rise of an integrated system of trade and political authority that unified thousands of such communities throughout the Midwest.

Hopewell interaction was grounded in common mortuary observances and the movement of exotic raw materials into the rural farmsteads where collective labor was elicited to construct earthen platforms and burial mounds. Materials and finished works recovered from Hopewell sites include sheet mica, copper, marine shell, silver, grizzly bear teeth, obsidian, woven cloth, carved stone pipes and finely decorated ceramic wares.

This effigy pipe was recovered in 1955 by Greg Perino, Gilcrease curator, during an archaeological excavation in central Illinois sponsored by the Thomas Gilcrease Foundation. Created from black steatite, the beaver figure incorporates the techniques of engraving, two-dimensional relief carving, and full form sculpting. From the base, or platform, the beaver figure assumes a fighting stance, evidenced by the tail tucked beneath the body. The beaver's incisors are carved from actual beaver teeth and skillfully inset to complete the defensive posture. Matched freshwater pearls are inset for eyes. This pipe has been called one of the greatest artworks to emerge from the great Hopewell cultural complex of the Americas.

+

HOPEWELL PLATFORM PIPE, CA. 200 CE
Pike County, Illinois
61.1140

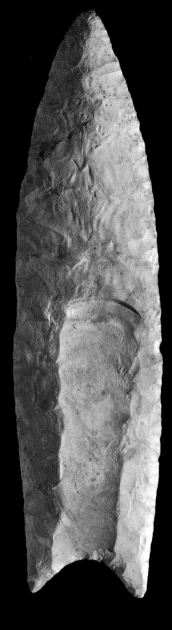

THIS LANCE POINT represents the more than 150,000 objects of chipped and ground stone that are curated in the Anthropology Department of Gilcrease Museum, and it is among the oldest objects in the collection. Following the migrations of game along the course of major waterways small bands of people used Clovis points to hunt mammoth, mastodon, and giant species of bear, moose and elk. Dating to 15,000 years ago, the Clovis point gains its name from the New Mexico town near which it was first discovered. Clovis points have been recovered in every continental state and Alaska, with similar points found in archaeological sites in Mexico and Central America.

Clovis points are distinguished by the fine workmanship of the blade and the unique manner in which the point was attached to a wooden handle. Clovis points had a long section of material removed through the use of a special pressure flaking technique in order to create a groove on one or both sides. This allowed the split end of the handle to seat well and provided a strong bond. This manner of hafting made possible a relatively thin shaft that allowed the projectile to penetrate deeply into game. Used for a relatively short period, the Clovis point was replaced by smaller fluted points, perhaps in response to a shift in the major game animals of the time.

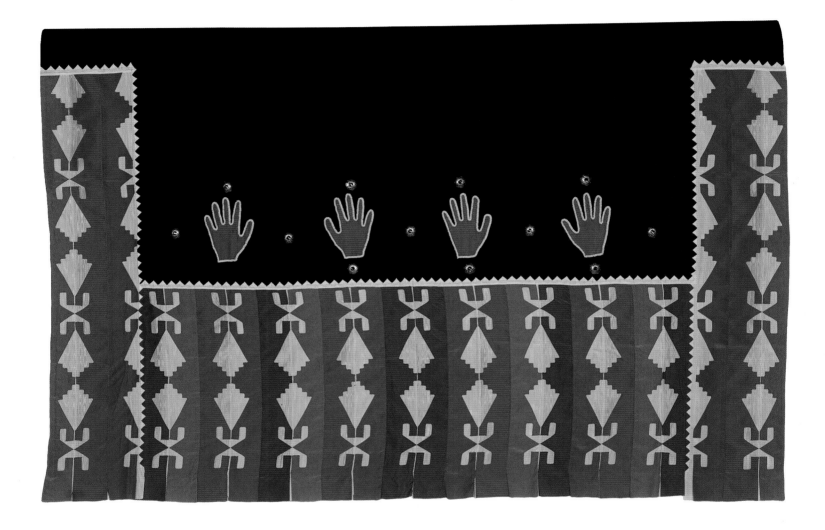

Fabric arts provide excellent examples of the incorporation of European trade goods into the traditional arts of Native Americans. In the hands of native artists, cloth and ribbon inspired the development of new techniques and applications, many of which are unique to North America. The decorative elements on this blanket are created in a reverse appliqué technique in which silk taffeta ribbons are sewn into layers with designs created by cutting and folding successive layers to partially reveal the different colored ribbons beneath. The Osage people maintain distinct patterns for use on male or female clothing and color combinations and design elements continue to convey both family and clan significance. Women's wearing blankets in the Osage community incorporate silhouettes of hands, hearts

and horses rendered in a single color of silk material that is outlined with one or more lanes of white beadwork. The addition of silver conches, worked in a Prairie style that emphasizes pierced cutouts as a major design technique, is a hallmark of classic Osage blankets.

Wearing blankets are important accoutrements to the traditional clothing worn by participants in the ceremonial and social dances of the Osage people. Heirloom examples are lovingly cared for and placed into service on special occasions, particularly during the annual Ilonshka dances that are held in June each year in the Gray Horse, Hominy, and Pawhuska communities.

+

OSAGE WEARING BLANKET, MID 20TH CENTURY

Osage County, Oklahoma

84.2960

THIS EFFIGY PIPE is relief carved from limestone in the form of a falcon holding a human head. Bird symbolism, of falcons in particular, is prominent in Mississippian art and mythology. Falcons and human-falcon impersonators are believed to have represented the chiefly and warrior elites in Mississippian society. Design images on marine shell engravings and copper repoussé plates portray the transformation of humans into falcons. Severed heads, a frequent motif in Mississippian art, are also associated with warriors and shamans, representing either an actual trophy head or a rattle in the form of a trophy head. The head motif may also symbolize the veneration of ancestors and leaders, particularly those of high rank and status.

This pipe was recovered at the Winterville Site, 150 miles south of Memphis, near Greenville, Mississippi. The site was occupied for centuries by Indian people who farmed and built mounds but were not integrated into the Mississippian system and its underlying cosmology. During a period of intense change in the 11th century CE, the site was quickly transformed into a major Mississippian center. Winterville grew into the largest Mississippian settlement in the Southeast region, becoming the source for the additional spread of the Mississippian worldview. At its height, the site contained at least twenty-three pyramidal mounds, a major temple mound at its center, and two massive plazas surrounded by lesser mounds and urban dwellings.

+

MISSISSIPPIAN EFFIGY PIPE, 1100 – 1200 CE

Washington County, Mississippi

61.1206

THE LAKOTA (SIOUX) people have a unique position in the history of Native American beadwork, largely based on the massive scale of their individual works and the sheer quantity in which they were produced. In the late 19th century, sedentary life on reservations, access to a regular supply of low cost, good quality seed beads, and the development of intricate geometric design elements coincided to fuel the intensification of beadwork in Lakota communities. In this style of Lakota beadwork, rows of beads are attached to the base material at each end, with parallel rows added to create "lanes." Lakota beadwork is characterized by a slight roll to the rows of beads created by adding more beads than will fit in the designated area.

This dress is constructed in the classic style of the Northern Plains, with the major portion of two hides used for the front and back of the skirt and another hide folded lengthwise to form the yoke. The natural form of the hide produces the distinct pattern of the sleeve openings. The yokes of Lakota dresses were generally fully beaded on background fields of white and blue with bold central design elements and pyramidal compositions. Dresses and accessories with this level of beaded decoration were reserved for important ceremonial and social events in the community.

An amulet in the shape of a lizard, decorated with beaded edging and covered in porcupine quill embroidery, is attached to the bottom of the yoke. The amulet contains the umbilical cord of a child, which was often hung from a cradleboard and later attached to an article of clothing to ensure good health and a long life.

+

LAKOTA DRESS WITH UMBILICAL CASE, LATE 19TH CENTURY
South Dakota
84.1795, 1796

POTTERY is one of the most enduring artifacts of the human experience. A natural extension of basketmaking, potterymaking began with the discovery that clay soils exposed to high heat are transformed into a hardened form. In the American Southwest, indigenous people created an incredible array of decorative forms and vessel types. So complete is this ceramic record that it is possible to construct highly detailed temporal and geographic sequences for their development and differentiation.

The Reserve style, named for the town of Reserve, New Mexico, begins with the introduction of a number of new design elements, including diagonal hatching, stepped terrace elements, and fine narrow lines. In later periods of Reserve style, the overall composition of the designs exhibited in this vessel was replaced with elements organized into horizontal bands. The painted designs on this piece incorporate symbols for corn (dots within a rectangle), the night sky (alternating white and black squares), rain (black dots in a band of white), and the earth (parallel lines).

This canteen is hand-formed using the coil and scrape method and baked at a relatively low temperature in a wood fire. The white background is created through the use of a slip, a layer of fine-grained clay applied to the vessel. The dark-colored design elements were painted on the surface using mineral pigments and a yucca fiber brush, and the surface of the completed vessel was finished with a fine polish.

+

RESERVE BLACK ON WHITE CANTEEN, 950 – 1,100 CE

Mogollon Rim, New Mexico

54.2687

Masks and their associated costumes are important elements in the religious and social lives of people around the world. Masking traditions in Mexico are the product of indigenous and European influences and are primarily associated with the dance performances held in conjunction with celebrations and festivals. In addition to face masks, the people of Mexico also create carved wooden figures that are worn around the waist. This piece is carved to represent the Caimán, or alligator, once common in many Mexican rivers. The legs of this Caimán are loosely attached to the body, allowing them to swing in response to the dancers movements and the hinged jaws are opened and closed through use of an attached string. The small opening in this piece would suggest that the intended wearer was a young boy.

This figure and its accompanying human face mask are worn during the performance of the Fisherman's Dance. The Fisherman's Dance involves a number of dancers who wear masks and carry nets. During the dance the Fishermen attempt to catch the Caimán in their nets. The dance is intended to increase the catch of fish, an important product in the local economies of many rural communities in Mexico. An additional figure in the form of a mermaid wearing a female face mask, long, flowing hair, and a carved wooden fish tail is sometimes incorporated into the Fisherman's Dance.

+

MEXICAN CAIMÁN FIGURE, MID 20TH CENTURY

Guerrero, Mexico

73.631

First documented on the Southern Plains in the 1860s, the lattice style cradleboard was widely used by the Kiowa, Comanche, and Cheyenne in Oklahoma. This style of cradle may have developed when travel by horse was diminished with permanent residence on reservations. The wooden lattice frame consists of two vertical slats that are connected with cross braces at the head and foot of the cradle. The longer, vertical slats are often trimmed to a point and decorated with metal tacks and ribbons. An understructure of formed rawhide produces a rigid shell that is wrapped in an elaborately decorated cover of hide, canvas or wool cloth.

Among the Kiowa people cradles were constructed and given to a new mother to celebrate the birth of her child and as a prayer for its health and happiness. The decorative detail of Kiowa cradles is highly distinctive in the use of diverse beadwork techniques and highly stylized abstract floral designs. Earlier examples are completely covered with beadwork while this cradle uses the red wool cloth of the cover as a background for the design elements. This cradle has been associated with Paukeigope (Etta Mopope), a noted Kiowa cradle maker and mother of Stephen Mopope, the celebrated Kiowa painter.

+

KIOWA LATTICE CRADLEBOARD, EARLY 20TH CENTURY

Oklahoma

84.663

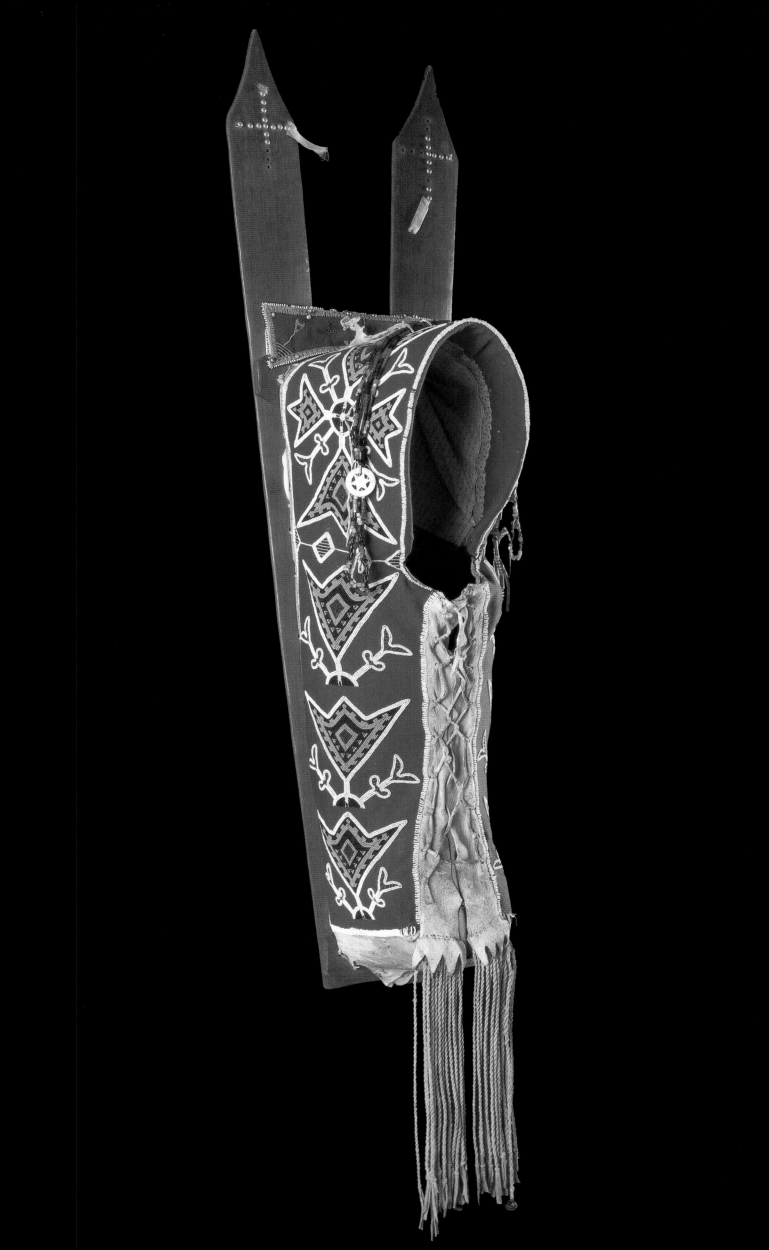

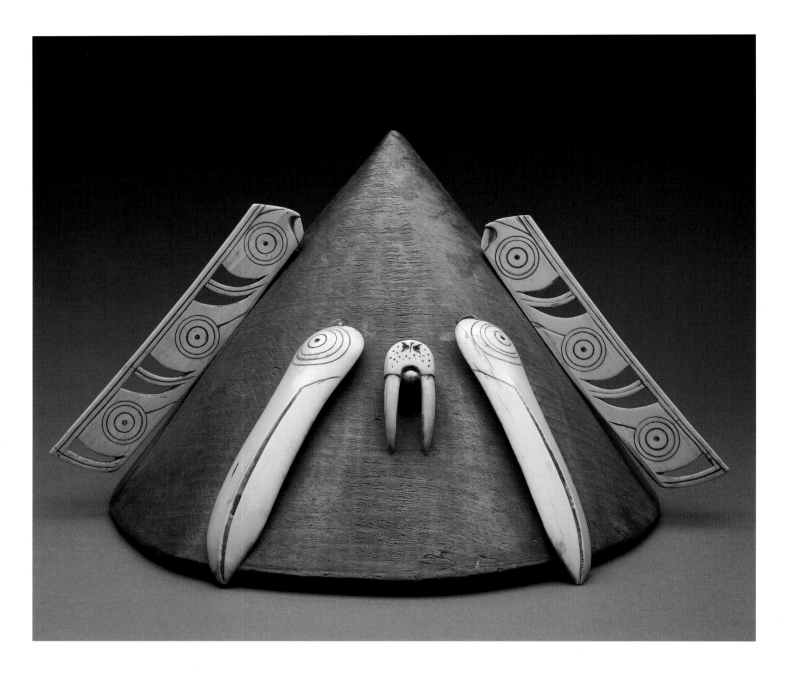

In spring and fall the Inuit people of coastal Alaska hunted seals as a major economic activity. Hunting from skin-covered kayaks with barbed harpoons, Inuit men used hunting hats, helmets, and visors to shade their eyes from the glare of snow, ice, and water. Seals were an important source of skins for warm clothing, meat and fat for food, lamp oil for a source of light, and waterproof garments constructed from the linings of internal organs.

Conical wooden hats were used throughout the central and southern coasts of the Bering Sea. The native people of the arctic region used spruce wood that was shaved thin and steamed so that it might be bent and shaped to construct boxes, trays, spoons, ladles, hats, and buckets. This hat uses a thinly carved piece of deer horn as a mending plate to secure the two edges of the cone at the back and is laced with twined vegetal fiber.

Hunting hats from the central coastal region of Alaska were usually adorned with a fairly standard configuration of ivory ornaments. Two carved and incised strips of ivory on the front of the hat represent the heads of gulls and cormorants. Positioned in the center of these strips is a carved animal head of a seal, walrus, sea otter, or other maritime mammal. The final decorative elements are two ivory "wings" attached to each side of the hat with stylized motifs that represent a bird head in profile.

+

NUNIVAK INUIT HUNTING HAT, LATE 19TH CENTURY

Nelson Island, Alaska

84.1321

Archaeological investigations of the Spiro Mounds Site have produced one of the greatest assemblages of pre-Columbian artwork north of Mexico. The majority of the artifacts recovered were objects of adornment, including beads, ear ornaments, gorgets and pendants. The raw material for most of these objects was whelk shell, a species of marine mollusk found in the Gulf of Mexico, the Florida Keys, and along the coast of Veracruz, Mexico. Shells were cut and ground into various shapes and embellished with engraved, carved, and cutout patterns and designs. The most common decorative technique was lineal engraving, probably with a pointed stone tool, with the bold lines filled with charcoal or mineral pigments.

Among the most spectacular objects from the Spiro site are shell cups recovered in large numbers from the burials of elites. The natural opening in the shell was enlarged by removing a portion of the spire with the resulting form opened as a cup by the removal of the internal columella. In most, the external shoulder spines are ground down and the entire exterior surface is smoothed to varying degrees. The engraved design on this cup consists of six human heads arranged in two groups. Details include depictions of a turban-like hairstyle, beaded forelocks, raccoon skin hair ornaments, and face paint around the eyes. The bands and crosshatching at the base of the shell probably represent a snake, an important symbol in Mississippian ceremonialism.

+

MISSISSIPPIAN SHELL CUP, 1200 – 1350 CE
Spiro Mounds Site, Oklahoma

90.385

THIS FIGURE PIPE is carved in the classic style of Cahokia, the great Mississippian center east of the modern-day city of St. Louis. Greater Cahokia included hundreds of temple mounds, great plazas, and an urban residence complex that at its height may have supported a population of 10,000 people. A large regional population grew corn on the rural floodplains of rivers and streams and hunted in the upland forests to support the core urban center. They were united through a political system based on ranked chiefdoms and a common religious ideology.

Human figure statues and pipes in the classic Cahokian tradition were sculpted from flint clays to represent male and female subjects identifiable as warriors, priests, and athletes.

This pipe depicts a male figure in a crouching position with a large hair bun on top of the head, shell, and bead ear ornaments and a raccoon skin headband. In his right hand, the figure holds a gourd rattle, a symbol of shamans, priests, and other religious specialists in Mississippian society. A snake form drapes around the figure's neck with its tail hanging down his chest. Serpent symbolism is prominent in Mississippian art and ideology and is believed to relate to efforts to insure the fertility of peoples and their crops. The discovery of this pipe in a late Woodland cultural context (1200-1350 CE) in the Illinois valley suggests that this piece continued to be revered long after the decline of Cahokia.

+

MISSISSIPPIAN FIGURE PIPE, 1100 — 1250 CE
Macoupin County, Illinois
61.18913

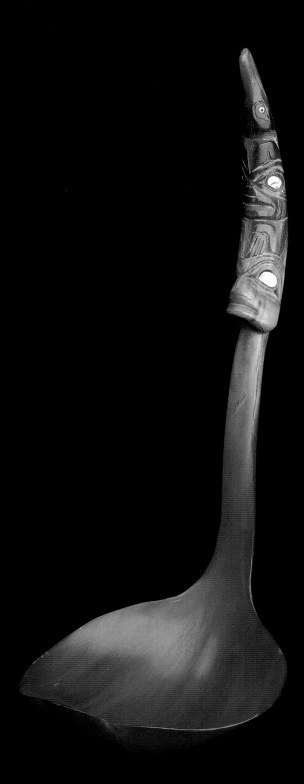

THE COAST SALISH people lived in numerous villages in the territory that is now southern British Columbia and northwestern Washington state. Their aboriginal economy was largely based on fishing for numerous species of salmon, collecting shellfish from tidal pools, and hunting for seals, sea lions, and occasionally whales. Trade with inland communities provided access to deer, elk, black bear, mountain goats, and sheep. The entire region provided an abundance of natural plants for food, medicine, and fibers.

The indigenous peoples of the Pacific Northwest incorporated the totemic crests of clans and lineages into their art. This practice was important in a society organized according to a rigid system of rank and status. Representational art was reflected in virtually every aspect of material culture, including, canoes, houses, clothing, musical instruments, storage boxes, and other household items. Spoons and ladles were carved from wood and the horns of Mountain sheep and goats. The horn was reduced to the general form of the spoon or ladle and then boiled or steamed until it became flexible. Afterwards it was placed in a two-piece wooden form where it was secured until it was dry. Handles and sometimes the undersides of bowls were carved and often embellished with shell inlay. The hosting of elaborate feasts was an important aspect of social and religious life and wealthy families maintained a number of bowls, platters, spoons and ladles that were carved in the crests of their lineage.

CENTRAL COAST SALISH LADLE, EARLY 20TH CENTURY
British Columbia, Canada
90.1829

The Library Collection

SARAH ERWIN

Thomas Gilcrease is known as having been a collector of Americana at a time when few others were interested in materials relating to the history of the Western Hemisphere. His library collection—which contains manuscripts, books, photographs, maps, imprints, and broadsides—expanded to include nearly 100,000 items.

Extensive travel to European museums and libraries during the 1920s and 1930s seems to have prompted Gilcrease's aspiration to create his own collection. Pride in his Native American heritage and interest in the history of the American West provided a focus for collecting activities. But the items chosen for inclusion in the library also demonstrate Gilcrease's belief that the history of America was not confined within the boundaries of the continental United States.

Gilcrease's library collection grew rapidly. While building it, he was not assisted by full-time advisors but would seek out single works as well as purchasing large groups of books or documents from dealers and other collectors.

Martin Wiesendanger in the Gilcrease library. Wiesendanger assisted in the opening and closing of the Thomas Gilcrease Museum in Texas and the opening of Gilcrease Museum in Tulsa.

+

In his biography of Thomas Gilcrease, David R. Milsten recounts an encounter between Gilcrease and book dealer Charles P. Everitt. Following several months of purchases from catalogues, the two men met, and Gilcrease admonished Everitt to remember that he always wished to purchase not only a first edition but also a fine copy of any book considered. Everitt proceeded to lecture Gilcrease that later and expanded editions could be much more important than simply a first edition. He recalled that Gilcrease smiled and responded, "I guess I shouldn't have said first edition. I should have said best edition."

Several large collections greatly increased the size of the Gilcrease library. In January 1944 Gilcrease agreed to purchase the entire collection of Philip G. Cole (1884–1941), to be delivered after the final payment three years later. In addition to the art, the collection included hundreds of books, portfolios, photographs, and illustrated letters from numerous artists. The focus of the Cole collection was western and Native American life. During the late 1940s, Gilcrease also acquired other important documents. Some of these came from the collection of Sir Thomas Phillipps (1792–1872), one of the greatest book collectors of all times. The dispersal of Phillipps's library after his death occurred in a series of sales that continued for the better part of a century. It was through a dealer and from the Phillipps estate that

Dr. and Mrs. Philip G. Cole riding on their estate near Tarrytown, New York ca. 1937.

Gilcrease purchased paintings, volumes, and extensive correspondence between the artist George Catlin and his sometime patron, Sir Thomas Phillipps. In 1948 Gilcrease obtained the majority of the Thomas Moran studio collection from the estate of Moran's daughter. Again, in addition to artworks, there were numerous journals, letters, and photographs.

In the early 1950s Gilcrease acquired some of the most notable documents in the library collection through the rare book and manuscript dealer Philip Rosenbach in Philadelphia. These included certified copies of the Declaration of Independence and Articles of Confederation, authorized by the Continental Congress and bearing the signatures of Benjamin Franklin and Silas Deane. The handwritten works were accompanied by a letter from the two American ambassadors to the Prussian minister Baron de Schulenburg and the latter's response. Gilcrease also purchased the volume including the first transcriptions of Christopher Columbus's own accounts of his voyages, written by Spanish curate Andres Bernaldes, as well as letters written by Diego Columbus and Hernando de Soto. Gilcrease's interest in Hispanic material continued into the early 1950s as he acquired the collection of George Robert Graham Conway (1837–1951). Conway, an Englishman living in Mexico, had for almost thirty years collected 16th– through 18th–century manuscripts relating to Spanish activities in the Western Hemisphere. These thousands of pages of documents were added to the library directly from the Conway estate.

Throughout his career as a collector, Gilcrease maintained an interest in the native peoples of the Americas. In 1946 he purchased a collection that included thousands of rare published items, many of which related to tribes that had been relocated to Indian

Territory. The collection had originally been assembled by Lester Hargrett (1902-1962). Hargrett was subsequently hired as director of the Gilcrease Foundation, a position he held until 1949. This collection, containing pamphlets, newspapers, broadsides, and government documents, is a tribute to Hargrett's skill as a collector and bibliographer. Because of Gilcrease's interest, however, the collection remains intact.

Even with the knowledge of the major groups of materials already mentioned, there remains little record of when or how Thomas Gilcrease obtained much of the material in the library. Extensive collections of the manuscripts of elected Cherokee chief John Ross and Choctaw leader Peter Pitchlynn are extremely important, yet no record of their acquisition exists. Similarly, it can only be assumed that Gilcrease was pleased to assemble the papers of Creek journalist and poet Alexander Posey. The lives of the two men had first crossed in a log cabin in the mid 1890s—Gilcrease in his first year of school and Posey in his first year as a teacher.

Expansion of the library special collections have continued, although at a slower pace, since the museum came under the guidance of the City of Tulsa in 1955. This growth has primarily been through donations. The 1964 acquisition of the studio collection of William R. Leigh, a gift from the artist's family, included numerous letters, scrapbooks, and photographs. In 1985 another artist's studio collection was bequeathed to the museum, that of Solomon McCombs. It represents the research and artwork of this Oklahoma artist of Muscogee-Creek heritage.

Life Magazine photo of Gilcrease with library materials, March 8, 1954.

In the early years, the library lacked in standard organization, but it never lacked in the interest of its founder. Many people who worked in the library as staff or as scholars discovered Gilcrease's amazing knowledge and appreciation of the material. He not only collected the books and documents but also studied them. The Gilcrease Museum Library does not comprise the largest body of materials relating to the history of the people, places, and events of the Americas. However, the special collections of unique or rare items that Gilcrease accumulated have preserved an important aspect of American history that might otherwise be lost.

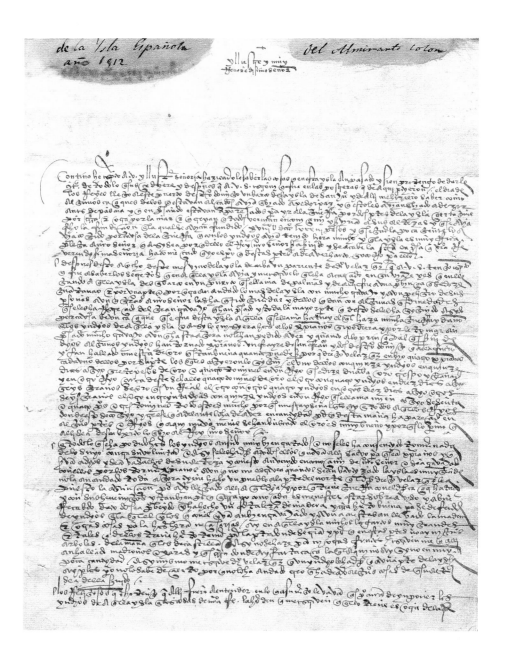

THIS LETTER, the oldest extant written from the Western Hemisphere, describes life on Hispaniola (later Haiti and the Dominican Republic) and Spanish activities in the new colonies under the rule of Diego Columbus. It also contains information about the earliest expedition to the island of Cuba. Diego Columbus (c. 1480/1526) was the eldest son of Christopher Columbus. In 1508 King Ferdinand of Spain appointed him Governor of the Indies, and for the remainder of his life he traveled between Spain and her colonies. As governor and later viceroy, Diego proved to be a just and capable ruler. His detractors, however, continually undermined his actions, often accusing him of wishing to become sovereign of the Indies.

In 1511 Columbus organized a troop of 300 men to travel to Cuba under the command of Diego Velazquez "to see what secrets lay there." In reporting upon the expedition, Columbus wrote, "The Island is very large, though they have not yet traversed it all. Now a town has sprung up in the north, to which Diego Velasquez, whom I have mentioned,

has given the name Asunción, through his having arrived there on Ascension Day. . . . there are no trees like those of Castile. . . . it is a land where big game/hunting is obtainable only upon a small scale." The letter is signed "El Almirante."

Diego addresses an appeal on behalf of the prestige of the Christian Church in America to the man most capable of favorably influencing the king in matters regarding the Spanish colonies: Cardinal Ximenez de Cisneros (1436/1517). The cardinal was a powerful person in Spain in the late 15th and early 16th centuries. His influence during the reign of Ferdinand and Isabella had far/reaching effects upon the early history of America. Queen Isabella went so far as to make a codicil to her will committing to the care of Cardinal Cisneros the native peoples of New Spain. Following the death of King Ferdinand and during the minority of Emperor Charles V, Cardinal Cisneros ruled Spain as sole Regent.

On the facing page is the signature of El Almirante.

+

DIEGO COLUMBUS Spanish, ca. 1480/1526
LETTER TO ARCHBISHOP CISNEROS, 1512

4075.67

... que ... segun ... deste almy[rante]? de la ysla ... en de

Ylluftte Señur

... ffetendi?ma senoza
... may noftas manos besa

m[uy] ... dalmy?ta?

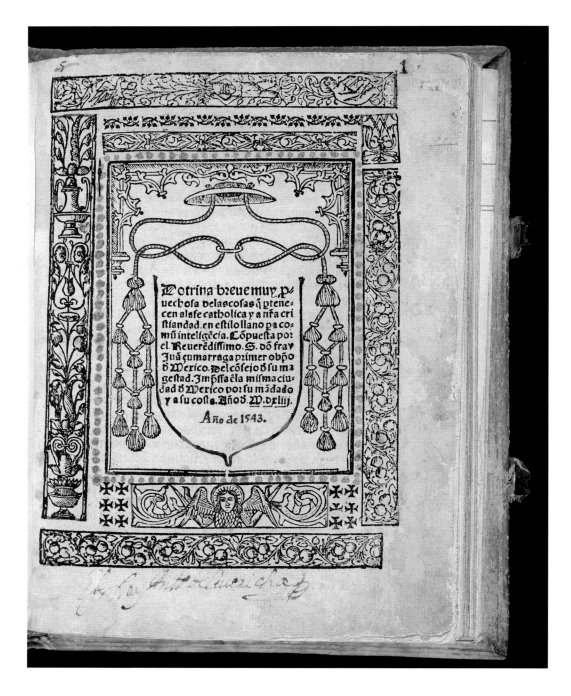

THE FIRST PRINTING PRESS in the Western Hemisphere was established in Mexico City in 1539, less than fifty years after the initial voyage of Columbus and within a hundred years of the invention of movable type. The earliest materials printed in the Americas were pamphlets, which were used until they wore out. By 1544 four volumes had been printed in Mexico City; of these the *Doctrina Cristiana* is believed to be the earliest extant. Printing was begun in the Spanish colonies in order to serve religious purposes. In the process of converting native populations to Christianity, it was necessary to have works such as catechisms, primers, and grammars in local languages. The early publications, both pamphlets and volumes, were documents of faith.

The job of establishing a press in the new Spanish colonies was awarded to Seville's foremost printer, Juan Cromberger. He selected Juan Pablos, an Italian printer working in Seville, to operate the new establishment. For several years works carried the imprint of Cromberger, after which Pablos operated the press under his own name. During the first decade of printing in Mexico, Pablos used paper and type from Spain. The paper was white, thin, opaque, and durable. The type featured semi-Gothic rounded letters that were heavy-faced and strong. Illustrations were enormously popular in early Mexican volumes. Title pages were designed to accommodate woodcuts, and a supply of Madonnas, saints, and devotional subjects developed. The title page of the *Doctrina Cristiana* attests its early publication with a peculiar assortment of mismatched borders. Around the inscription the clerical hat (a *galero*) and hat strings with ten tassels tell us that this volume was produced at the direction of an archbishop. Bindings at this time were utilitarian. Most were vellum, made from durable and inexpensive sheepskin.

During the colonial era Mexico was the center of printing in Spain's empire. Despite strict censorship and legal restrictions, more than 1,700 works were printed in Mexico City between 1739 and the end of the 17th century.

+

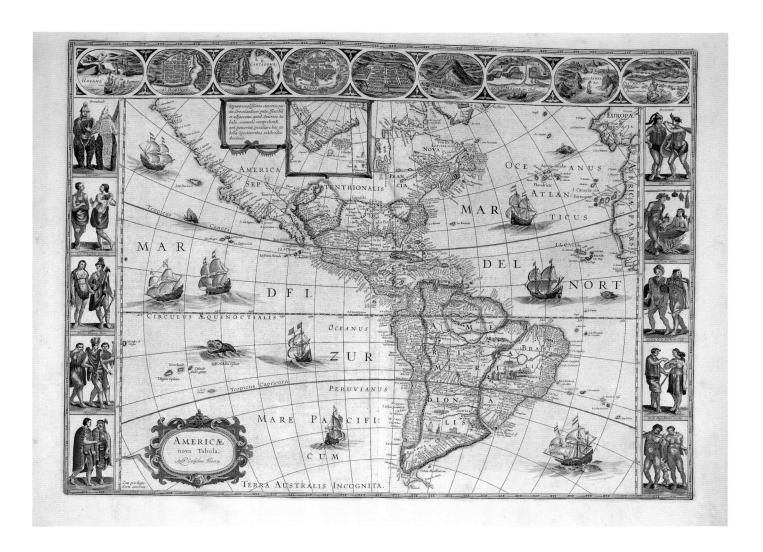

EARLY MAPS illustrate both the history of discovery and the history of art. They provide a constantly changing and attractive record of what people believed about the physical world. To enjoy early maps, one should consider them in their historical context. Exploration and encounter provided details and increased awareness of the shape and character of distant lands. As art, the design of maps developed with time, as did the style in which the hand coloring was applied. The distinctive palettes of each age and country also aided in interpreting the map itself.

Willem Janszoon Blaeu (1571-1638) and his son Joan were part of the Golden Age of the Republic of the United Netherlands. This publication of the House of Blaeu illustrates its high standards of geographical knowledge and cartography as well as the arts of papermaking, printing, engraving, and binding. The elder Blaeu wrote in 1636 that he intended to describe the entire world in a multivolume set of atlases. Almost thirty years later, his son Joan Blaeu

succeeded in doing so in the *Atlas Maior,* which appeared in Dutch, German, Latin, and French editions. A Spanish edition was being prepared when the printing shop was destroyed by fire in 1672. The atlases were available in yellow vellum binding with gold tooling, morocco leather, and purple velvet. Blaeu's *Atlas Maior* was the most expensive printed book available in the latter half of the 17th century. It was designed for those with both the material and intellectual resources required to buy and appreciate it, and it was a traditional gift presented on behalf of the Netherlands to royal and important personages.

The Gilcrease collection includes a complete set of twelve volumes of the French edition. The pictures bordering the map of North America reveal the European concept of the inhabitants of the northern hemisphere. Bound in vellum and containing hand-colored maps, these were formerly owned by the House of Liechtenstein.

+

JOAN BLAEU Flemish, 1596-1673
ATLAS MAIOR, AMERICA, 1663

3976.31

THEODOR DE BRY (1528-1598) created some of the earliest and most influential illustrations of native peoples of the Western Hemisphere. Throughout the 17th and 18th centuries, the general population of Europe viewed the newly encountered and exotic Americas through images that de Bry produced and later publishers often replicated. Working from original accounts and artwork, de Bry made copperplate engravings that provided a contemporary view of detailed scenes of American clothing and culture. He also illustrated episodes in the history of European contact and the often-resulting conflict. The images, however, are not totally accurate as de Bry used European standards for figure types and landscape.

Born into an affluent Protestant family in the Netherlands, de Bry become a goldsmith and engraver but fled the region in the early 1570s to escape religious persecution. In 1589 he rejoined his family, which had resettled in Frankfurt and established a publishing business.

Beginning in 1590, de Bry and his sons illustrated a series of travel literature volumes in which narratives purchased from English, Dutch, French, Italian, and Spanish sources were reissued with de Bry's illustrations. The first in the series was Thomas Hariot's narrative detailing the English settlement in a place called Virginia. The following year a similar volume was published offering an account of the

earliest French attempt to establish a colony in Florida. The settlement, established near the St. Johns River in 1564, lasted little more than a year before it was destroyed by the Spanish. One of the colony's few survivors was the artist Jacques Le Moyne de Morgues. Sent as an official artist and cartographer, Le Moyne documented many aspects of the life of the Timucua people. De Bry's drawing on the page shown here illustrates Le Moyne's account of how alligators, a food source for the Timucua, were killed by driving a long pole down their throats.

The publications continued beyond de Bry's death in 1598 and eventually included voyages to Asia as well as the Americas.

Theodor de Bry's engraving of the town of Secota (facing page) was based on a watercolor by John White, a member of the group sent by Sir Walter Raleigh to found an English colony on Roanoke Island in 1585. Located near what are now the Outer Banks of North Carolina, the Secotans lived in permanent villages, farming collectively during the growing season and dispersing to hunt in the winter. Crops depicted are tobacco, sunflowers, pumpkins, and maize in three stages of growth. The buildings are family dwellings, storehouses, and (upper right) a hut with a watchman to frighten animals away from the crops.

+

THEODOR DE BRY Flemish, 1528-1598
ALLIGATOR HUNT AND INDIAN VILLAGE OF SECOTA
2475.154

TB   20

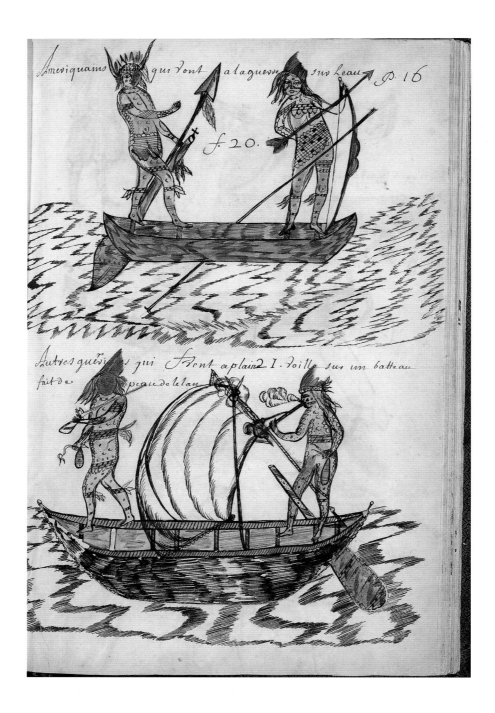

THE *Codex Canadiensis* contains some of the earliest original drawings relating to New France, now known as Canada. Created in the 17th century, the 180 watercolor and ink sketches in this volume represent several tribes of native peoples as well as flora and fauna in the Great Lakes region. The drawings are somewhat naïve but are relatively accurate in detail compared to other illustrations of the period. The binding, which bears the coat of arms of the King of France, attests to the fact that the Codex was at one time in the royal collection.

Louis Nicolas, the author and illustrator of the *Codex Canadiensis*, joined the Jesuit Order with the intention of coming to North America as a missionary. He arrived in Quebec in 1664 and did not return to France until 1674. Although not reputed to be a refined man, he had the persistence of a scholar and recorded detailed information concerning the newly encountered region. Working among the Ottawa and Mohawk peoples, Nicolas collected plant specimens that were later transplanted into the botanical gardens at Montpellier.

Upon his return to France, Nicolas devoted himself to preparing for publication a manuscript with illustrations. His manuscript, entitled *Trait de anumauz quatre pieds terrestres et amphibies que se trouvent dan les Indes occidentals ou Amerique septrentrionale*, presumably was prepared at the same time as most of the illustrations that are now known as *Codex Canadiensis*. Upon the rejection of his first manuscript for publication, Nicolas prepared a more polished version entitled *Historie naturelle; ou la fidelle recherché de tout ce qu'il ya a de rare dan les Indes occidentals*. Nicolas's downfall, however, seemed to have been caused by his gruff manners and fits of temper. In 1678 he was dismissed from the Jesuit Order. None of Nicolas's works was ever published.

+

LOUIS NICOLAS French, 17th century
CODEX CANADIENSIS, 1674/80

4726.7

Michinenh petite tortue

p.39.

micipichiKoule
dieu de l'eaux selon
les Americains

56

Michinak grande tortue de l'Isle
de s.t HElaine qui est si grande qu'on fait
L'Imperialle 2 dun grand carosse

1

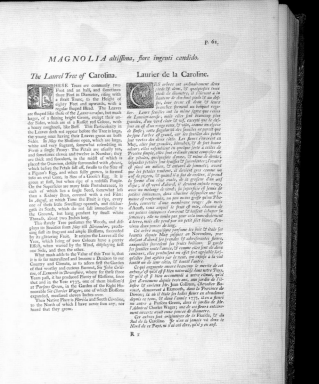

MARK CATESBY (1682–1749) was one of the first to undertake a systematic investigation of the plant and animal life of the British colonies in North America. The naturalist traveled from 1712 to 1719, studying in Virginia and the Appalachian Mountains and journeying as far as Jamaica. On a second expedition to America in 1722, he lived in Charleston, South Carolina, and traveled to Florida, Georgia, and the Bahamas. Upon returning to England in 1726, Catesby started compiling text and illustrations for the two-volume set *A Natural History of Carolina, Florida, and the Bahamas*. It was issued by subscription, the first volume being completed in November 1732 (although the dated given on the title pages is 1731), and the second in 1743. The appendix to the second volume was not issued until 1747. Although Catesby had done extensive research, he also drew upon the work of natural historian John Lawson and artist-explorer John White. Well-known in 18th century England and America, Catesby was elected a Fellow in the Royal Society in recognition of his work.

The two-volume set, over twenty years in the making, includes 220 plates illustrating 171 plants, 109 birds, 46 fish, 33 amphibians and reptiles, 31 insects, and nine quadrupeds. The text contains descriptions of climate, agriculture, and soil as well as an essay on native peoples of the regions. It was the first work to feature color plates of the subjects. Catesby produced the majority of the plates himself but was assisted on the second volume by George Dennis Ehret (1708–1770). Ehret, born in Germany, was highly regarded as a botanical illustrator and in 1757 was elected to the Royal Society.

Shown on the facing page is one of four original watercolors of the magnolia that Ehret executed and the engraving of the magnolia that was used in *A Natural History of Carolina, Florida, and the Bahamas*. Although eventually overshadowed by John James Audubon, Catesby was a pioneer in scientific illustration. For a century his was the best illustrative set of the flora and fauna of North America.

Magnolia; Altissima Lauro-Cerasi folio, flore ingenti candido. CATESB:

G. D. Ehret.

+

GEORGE EHRET German, 1708-1770

MAGNOLIA CREATED FOR A NATURAL HISTORY OF CAROLINA, FLORIDA, AND THE BAHAMAS

0276.1622

NEW
PRINCIPLES
OF
GARDENING:

Or, The Laying out and Planting

PARTERRES, GROVES, WILDERNESSES, LABYRINTHS, AVENUES, PARKS, &c.

After a more GRAND and RURAL MANNER, than has been done before;

With Experimental Directions
For raising the several Kinds of FRUIT-TREES, FOREST-TREES, EVER-GREENS and FLOWERING-SHRUBS with which Gardens are adorn'd.

To which is added,

The various NAMES, DESCRIPTIONS, TEMPERATURES, MEDICINAL VIRTUES, USES and CULTIVATIONS of several ROOTS, PULSE, HERBS, &c. of the Kitchen and Physick Gardens, that are absolutely necessary for the Service of Families in general.

Illustrated with great Variety of GRAND DESIGNS, curiously Engraven on twenty eight Folio Plates, by the best Hands.

By *BATTY LANGLEY* of *Twickenham.*

LONDON:
Printed for A. BETTESWORTH and J. BATLEY in *Pater-Noster Row*; J. PEMBERTON in *Fleetstreet*; T. BOWLES in St. *Paul's Church-Yard*; J. CLARKE, under the *Royal Exchange*; and J. BOWLES at *Mercer's Hall* in *Cheapside.*
M DCC.XXVIII.

Batty Langley's *New Principles of Gardening* is closely associated with George Washington's life at Mount Vernon. Washington ordered the book in May 1759, only months after he had married Martha Dandridge Custis. He mentions his recent receipt of New Principles of Gardening, along with other new books and items from England, in a diary entry dated January 2, 1760. It was probably on this date that Washington wrote his name, the year, and the price paid for the volume on the title page. Washington, who inherited Mount Vernon, toiled for forty-five years to improve and enlarge the estate. In developing the master plan for the Mount Vernon grounds, he employed many of the patterns provided in New Principles of Gardening.

Batty Langley (1696-1751), a pioneer of British landscape gardening, produced more than twenty volumes of architecture and garden design. His publications were well known in colonial America, and his ideas had widespread influence. *New Principles of Gardening* was published in 1728 and remained popular for decades. The volume opens with a discussion of geometry in landscape architecture and continues with principles of garden design. There are chapters concerning forest, evergreen trees, and shrubs. A final segment contains the design of a proper kitchen garden containing vegetables, herbs, and medicinal plants. The volume includes twenty-eight folding plates depicting model gardens. These patterns illustrated Langley's preference for the appearance of natural simplicity, with curving paths and meandering walks. In looking at the grounds at Mount Vernon, it is evident that Washington relied upon Langley's theories of design.

+

BATTY LANGLEY English, 1696-1751
NEW PRINCIPLES OF GARDENING
3276.167

PRINTED DOCUMENTS known as broadsides or broadsheets usually consist of a single page and are designed to relay information to a wide audience. The content of a broadside might range from an official proclamation to an ordinary advertisement. The earliest broadsides appeared soon after the invention of the printing press in the middle of the 15th century. For the next 200 years broadsides became very popular, providing an inexpensive method to reach the general population.

In England broadsides were commonly used to record events and publicize opinions. By the 18th century they provided entertainment in the form of satirical or humorous ballads and poems and served as a forum in which complex ideas were debated. Broadsides appeared in the American colonies as soon as printing presses arrived, with colonial uses continuing the rich traditions that had developed in England. By the 19th century the form of broadsides had changed. Debates common during earlier times gave way to condensed and highly punctuated text. Stylistically, typefaces became bolder and more decorative.

The three broadsides from the Gilcrease collection that follow include a humorous song, a diatribe against the "bloody deeds" of Andrew Jackson, and an exhortation to potential white settlers of Indian Territory.

In 1762 a delegation of Cherokee leaders traveled to England to be presented to King George III. The group included the British Lieutenant Henry Timberlake, an interpreter who died on the voyage to England, and three Cherokees. Cunne Shote, also identified as Standing Turkey, Tohanohawighton, who was called Pouting Pigeon, and Ostenaco, known as The Mankiller, were in England about two months. The group was extremely popular and was often followed by large crowds while touring London. *A New*

Humorous Song On The Cherokee Chiefs Inscribed to the Ladies of Great Britain depicts their exotic dress, hairstyles and tattooing. It also mocks the interest shown by the English ladies in the Cherokees.

Andrew Jackson's fame originated from his military exploits. In 1814 Jackson commanded the Tennessee volunteers and defeated the Creeks at the Battle of Horseshoe Bend. This victory brought him a commission as a major general in the United States army and placed him against British forces as protector of New Orleans. During these campaigns Jackson offered little leniency, on several occasions punishing misdeeds among his own troops with executions. His harshness was widely publicized, as in the broadside entitled *Some Accounts of the Bloody Deeds of General Jackson*, and was recounted nearly ten years later, when Jackson sought the presidency.

The Oklahoma Colony was established by David L. Payne to promote settlement on land in Indian Territory. Payne, a Civil War veteran and briefly a Kansas legislator, was a charismatic organizer who gave the land movement almost a religious tone. He sold thousands of Oklahoma Colony memberships, promising associates superior sections of land. Colony members were encouraged to assemble in camps in southern Kansas and northern Texas, from which Payne staged several invasions into Indian Territory. The settlers ware always expelled by the U.S. Cavalry, but the continued agitation maintained pressure on the federal government. Handbills like the one proclaiming Oklahoma Colony! advertised the benefits of colonization to potential settlers.

+

The Stalking Turkey

The Pouting Pidgeon

The Man killer

A NEW HUMOROUS SONG,

ON THE

CHEROKEE CHIEFS.

Inscribed to the LADIES of GREAT BRITAIN.

By H. HOWARD.

To the Tune of, *Cæsar and Pompey were both of them Horned.*

I.

WHAT a Piece of Work's here, and a d—d Botheration !
Of Three famous Chiefs from the *Cherokee* Nation ;
Who the Duce wou'd ha' thought, that a People polite, Sir,
Wou'd ha' ftir'd out o' Doors to ha' feen fuch a Sight, Sir ?
Are M——rs fo rare in the *Britifh* Dominions,
That we thus fhou'd run crazy for *Canada Indians.*
          Are M——rs fo rare, &c.

II.

How eager the Folks at *Vauxhall*, or elfewhere, Sir,
With high Expectation and Rapture repair, Sir ;
Tho' not one of them all can produce the leaft Reafon,
Save that M——rs of all Sorts are always in Seafon.
If fo, let the Chiefs here awhile have their Station,
And fend for the whole of the *Cherokee* Nation.
          If fo, let the Chiefs, &c.

III.

The Ladies, dear Creatures, fo fqueamifh and dainty,
Surround the great *Canada* Warriors in plenty ;
Wives, Widows and *Matrons*, and pert litttle *Miffes*,
Are preffing and fqueezing for *Cherokee* Kiffes.
Each grave looking Prude, and each fmart looking Belle, Sir,
Declaring, no *Englifhman* e'er kifs'd fo well, Sir.
          Each grave looking Prude, &c.

IV.

That *Cherokee* Lips are much fofter and fweeter,
Their Touch more refin'd, and their Kiffes repleter,
The fair ones agree—nay, I mean not to flatter,
For who like the Ladies can judge of the Matter ?
Ye Nymphs then, who like 'm, indulge your odd Paffion,
Be fw——d by the Chiefs of the *Cherokee* Nation.
          Ye Nymphs then, &c.

V.

Ye Females of *Britain*, fo wanton and witty,
Who love even Monkies, and fwear they are pretty ;
The *Cherokee* Indians, and ftranger *Shimpanzeys*,
By Turns, pretty Creatures, have tickl'd your Fancies ;
Which proves, that the Ladies fo fond are of Billing,
They'd kifs even M——rs, were M——rs as willing.
          Which proves, that, &c.

VI.

No more then thefe Chiefs, with their fcalping Knives dread, Sir,
Shall ftrip down the Skin from the *Englifhman*'s Head, Sir ;
Let the Cafe be revers'd, and the Ladies prevail, Sir,
And inftead of the Head, fkin the *Cherokee* T—l, Sir.
Ye bold Female *Scalpers*, courageous and hearty,
Collect all your Force for a *grand Scalping Party.*
          Ye bold Female Scalpers, &c.

VII.

For Weapons, ye Fair, you've no need to petition,
No Weapons you'll want for this odd Expedition ;
A foft Female Hand, the beft Weapon I wean is,
To ftrip down the Bark of a *Cherokee* P—s.
Courageous advance then, each fair *Englifh* Tartar,
Scalp the *Chiefs* of the *Scalpers*, and give them no Quatter.
          Courageous advance then, &c.

Sold by the AUTHOR, oppofite the Union Coffee-Houfe, in the Strand, near Temple-Bar, and by all the Print and Pamphlet-fellers.
[PRICE SIX-PENCE.]
N. B. In a few Days will be publifhed the *Political Bagpiper.* A new Song, with a Head-piece.

Some Account of some of the Bloody Deeds OF GENERAL JACKSON.

A brief account of the Execution of the Six Militia Men.

As we may soon expect to have the *official* documents in relation to the SIX MILITIA MEN, arrested, tried, and put to death, under the orders of General Andrew Jackson, this may not be an improper time to give to the public some of the particulars of their execution, as we have them from "AN EYE WITNESS," who appeals to Col. Russell, for the truth of every word he relates.

—

Harris was a Baptist preacher, with a large family. He had hired as a substitute for three months. This was the case with most of them. They were ignorant men, but obstinate in what they believed right, and what they had been told by their officers was right.—They were all sure they could not be kept beyond three months, and they gave up their musquets, and had provisions dealt out to them, from the public stores, before they left the camp.—This confirmed their convictions that they were right and doing what was lawful.

Col. Russel commanded at the execution. The Militia men were brought to the place in a large wagon. The military dispositions being made, Col. Russell rode up to the wagon and ordered the men so descend. Harris was the only one who betrayed feminine weakness. The awfulness of the occasion; his wife and nine children; the parting with his son; and the fear of a quickly approaching ignominious death! quite overcome him, and he sunk in unmanly grief. No feeling of military pride could brace him up.

Col. Russel, doubtless, felt as a man, but he felt also for the pride of the army, and desired to animate the men with fortitude. "You are about to die, "said he, by the sentence of a Court "Martial—die like men; *like soldiers.* "You have been brave in the field—"you have fought well—do no discredit to your country, or dishonour to the "army, or yourselves, by any unmanly "fears. Meet your fate with courage."

Harris attempted to make some apology for his conduct, but while he spoke, he wept bitterly. The fear of death, the idea that he should never again behold his wife and little ones, and his son weeping near him, had taken such entire possession of his mind that it was impossible he should rally.

Lewis, the gallant Lewis, said in a clear and manly tone, "Colonel, I have "served my country well. I love it "dearly, and would, if I could, serve "it longer and better. I have fought "bravely—*you know* I have, and HERE "I have a right to say so MYSELF. I "would not wish to die in this way"—here his voice faltered, and he passed the back of his right hand over his eyes—"I did not expect it: But, I am now "as firm as I have been in battle, and "you shall see that I will die as be"comes a soldier, you know I am a "brave man." "Yes, Lewis, said the Colonel, you have always behaved like a brave man." Other sentences were uttered, other declarations were made, and words of comfort spoken, but they were lost on me: my attention, says an Eye Witness, being chiefly directed to Lewis.

Six coffins were ranged as directed, and on each of them knelt one of our condemned American Militia Men—Such a sight was never seen before! I trust to God it never will be seen again! Six soldiers were detailed and drawn up to fire at each man. What an awful duty! Their white caps were drawn over the faces of the unhappy men.—Harris evidently trembled, and I could almost persuade myself that the heart of Lewis was enlarged, and that his bosom rose with manly courage to meet death. The fatal word was given and they all fell.

As we approached the scene of blood and carnage, Lewis gave signs of life; the rest were all dead—he crawled upon his coffin. After the lapse of a few minutes he said—I give his very words: "Colonel"—the Colonel was close to him—"Colonel, I am not killed, but I am sadly cut and mangled." His body was now examined and it was found that but four balls had wounded him. "Colonel," said he, "did I behave well." "Yes, Lewis"—said the Colonel in the kindest tone of voice—"like a man." "Well sir," said he, "have I not atoned for this offence? *Shall I not live?*" The Colonel was much agitated, and gave orders that the Surgeon should, if possible, preserve his life. They did all that skill and humanity could do—it was all of no avail. Poor Lewis expressed a great desire to live—"not," said he at one time, "that I fear death, "but I would repent me of some sins, "and I desire to live yet a little long"er in the world." He suffered inconceivable agony, from his wounds, and died on the fourth day.

Many a soldier has wept over his grave. He was a brave man and much beloved. He suffered twenty deaths.—I have seen the big drops chase each other down his forehead with pain and anguish. There was much sensibility and sympathy throughout the camp.—I would not have, unjustly and unnecessarily, signed this death warrant for all the wealth of all the Indies. The soldiers detailed to shoot Lewis had, from strong feelings of sympathy, or mistaken humanity failed to shoot him—but four balls had entered his body.

"An Eye Witness" appeals to Col. Russell, who he thinks now lives in Alabama, for the perfect truth of this sketch. He does not fear but the Colonel will keenly recollect and faithfully depict the horrors of the day on which six Americans were shot to death under his command—but not by his orders.

The order bears date the very day after *General Jackson* returned in triumph to New Orleans, and the day before he joyfully went, under triumphal arches, to the Temple of the living God; where, says the historian, "they *crowned* their adored General with laurels." The order for the execution of these six unhappy men bears date January 22, 1815. His crown of laurels had not yet withered, when blood, the life's blood of his countrymen, of his fellow soldiers, flowed plentifully by his order. May that order and its consequences, sink deep into the hearts of the American people and steel them against him who had no flesh in his obdurate heart; who did not feel for Man; in the midst of Joy and Revelry, almost in the more immediate presence of his Creator, who issued the fatal order to put his fellow creatures to death, and to make their wives & children, widows and orphans.

MOURNFUL TRAGEDY;

Or, the death of Jacob Webb, David Morrow, John Harris, Henry Lewis, David Hunt, & Edward Lindsey—six militia men, who were condemned to die, the sentence approved by Major General JACKSON, and by his order the whole six shot.

O! DID you hear that plaintive cry
Borne on the southern breeze?
Saw you JOHN HARRIS earnest pray
For mercy, on his knees?

Low to the earth he bent, and pray'd
For pardon from his chief;
But to his earnest prayer for life
JACKSON, alas! was deaf.

"Spare me"—he said—"I mean no wrong,
"My heart was always true:
"Frist for my county's cause it beat,
"And next, great Chief, for you.

"We thought our time of service out—
"Thought it our right to go:
"We meant to violate no law,
"Nor wish'd to shun the foe.

"Our officers declared that we
"Had but three months to stay;
"We served those three months faithfully,
"Up to the latest day.

"No one suspects intended wrong;
"The judgment only erred:
"In such a case, O noble Chief,
"Let mercy's voice be heard.

"At home an aged mother waits
"To clasp her only son;
"A wife, and little children—this arm
"Alone depend upon.

"Cut me not off from these dear ties;
"So soon from life's young bloom;
"O 'tis a dreadful thing to die,
"And moulder in the tomb!

"Sure mercy is a noble gem
"On every Chieftain's brow;
"More sparkling than a diadem—
"O exercise it now.—"

'Twas all in vain, John Harris' pary'r,
'Tis past the soul's belief!
Hard as the flint was Jackson's heart;
He would not grant relief.

He order'd Harris out to die,
And five poor fellows more!
Young, gallant men, in prime of life,
To welter in their gore!!

Methinks I hear the muffled drum,
And see the column move;
—Lo here they come—how sad their looks:
Farewell to life and love!

See six black coffins rang'd along—
Six graves before them made;
Webb, Lindsey, Harris, Lewis, Hunt,
And Morrow kneeled and prayed.

They kneel'd and pray'd, and tho't of home,
And all its dear delights.
The deadly tubes are levell'd now—
The scene my soul affrights!

Sure he will spare! Sure JACKSON you
Will all reprive but one—
O hark! those shrieks! that cry of death!
The dreadful deed is done!

All six militia men were shot;
And O! it seems to me
A dreadful deed—a bloody act
Of needless cruelty.

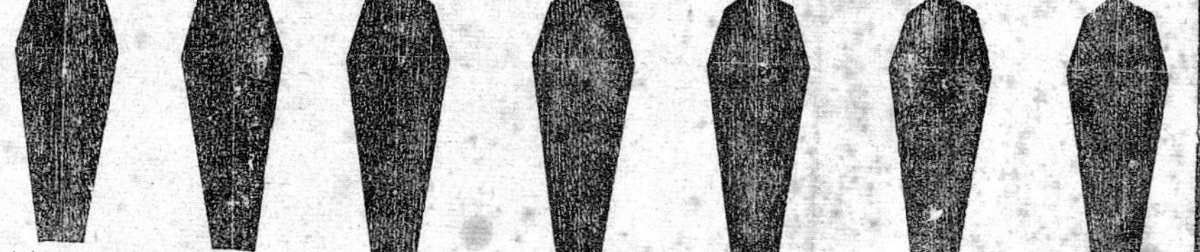

A short time before the execution of the militia-men, seven regular soldiers were shot near Nashville, by a band of regulars scarcely sufficient to guard the prisoners.—They were confined in a house, and taken out and executed one at a time, there being scarcely enough men for the purpose of executing and guarding at the same moment. An eighth soldier was to have been executed at the same time. He was a young man, who had deserted one month before his time had expired. General Jackson doomed him to die with the others. He was saved by a writ of habeas corpus from Judge M'Nairy, who fell under Jackson's displeasure for snatching this one victim from his blood-stained hands. If Jackson's army had been at hand, no doubt M'Nairy would have shared the fate of Judge Hall and Judge Fromentin. Capital punishments in an army, are designed for example as well as for penalty; but in this case it was a transaction of horror to peaceful citizens: no army was there to witness the bloody tragedy. He has ever been a man of "blood and carnage."

Do not be startled, gentle reader, at the picture before you. It is all true and every body ought to know it. Gen. Jackson having made an assault upon Samuel Jackson, in the streets of Nashville, & the latter not being disposed to stand still and be beaten, stooped down for a stone to defend himself. While in the act of doing so, Gen. Jackson drew the sword from his cane and run it through Samuel Jackson's body, the sword entering his back and coming out of his breast. For this offence an indictment was found against Genl. Jackson, by a grand jury, upon which he was subsequently arraigned and tried. But finding means to persuade the petit jury that he committed the act in self-defence, he was acquitted. Gentle reader, it is for you to say, whether this man, who carries a sword cane, and is willing to run it through the body of any one who may presume to stand in his way, is a fit person to be our President.

Poor JOHN WOODS; he was a generous hearted, noble fellow as ever lived, who had volunteered in the service of his country. He was on guard one day at Fort Strother—the officer of the guard had permitted him to go to his tent, and snatch a hasty breakfast; whilst disposing of his scanty meal, seated on the ground beside his skillet, an upstart little officer, who was not Woods' equal at home, ordered him to pick up and carry off some bones that lay scattered about the place—Woods refused, and the little officer attempted to compel him. At this instant, Gen. Jackson, having heard the dispute, came out of his tent, and without knowing any thing of the merits of the case, repeatedly vociferated—'*Shoot the damn'd rascal!—Shoot the damn'd rascal.*' For this offence, the unfortunate, the gallant Woods, was tried, condemned and shot. Before his trial, Gen. Jackson used this language to the court-martial. "*By the immortal God! if you find him guilty I will not pardon him!*" And he kept his promise; though he did offer a pardon provided he would enlist in the regular service—Thus perished as noble a fellow as ever lived, for as trifling an offence as ever took the life of man!!!

On the 27th day of March, 1814, General Jackson had found at an Indian village, at the bend of the Tallapousie, about 1000 Indians, with their *squaws* and *children*, "running about among their huts." The following is an account of the sanguinary massacre which took place;—it is Gen. Jackson's own, and therefore must be received as sufficient evidence against himself. He says:—"DETERMINING TO EXTERMINATE them, I detached Gen. Coffee with the mounted men, and nearly the whole of the Indian force, early on the morning of yesterday, to cross the river about two miles below the encampment, and to surround the bend in such a manner as that none of them should escape by attempting to cross the river." The result he then details:—"*Five hundred and fifty seven were left dead on the Peninsula, and a great number of them were killed by the horsemen in attempting to cross the river*; IT IS BELIEVED THAT NO MORE THAN TEN ESCAPED. WE CONTINUED to DESTROY *many of them who had concealed themselves under the banks of the river, until we were prevented by the night.* THIS MORNING WE KILLED 16 WHICH HAD BEEN CONCEALED."

We ask you to pause and reflect that the above tragic narration of cold-blooded and merciless cruelty, is taken from an official communication made by General Andrew Jackson.

The General, after sleeping (with what composure, we cannot say) thro' the night ensuing the tragedy we speak of, awoke in the morning surrounded by the corpses of "five hundred and seventy" fellow creatures, to cause, by way of worthy afterpiece, sixteen others to be dragged from their concealments, and put to death in cold blood. We cannot boast of more than common sensibility, but we must think that to witness such an act, would make ours a little cold also. What are the general's words?—these: "this morning we killed sixteen which had been concealed"—and the man who acts and speaks thus; who has half as much blood upon his conscience, as he has upon his hands,—he, forsooth, is to be called the peer and *like* of Washington, the happy warrior,—

——————"he
Whom every man at arms could wish to be!"

But it is time to have done with the unpleasant subject. We will observe in addition to the details already given, that the village was burnt, and several women and children killed. In conclusion, we ask our fellow citizens, whether Genl. Jackson, though he has contributed largely to the military reputation of our country, has not done enough to disqualify him, in the eyes of the people as virtuous as they are free, for the office he seeks at their hands.

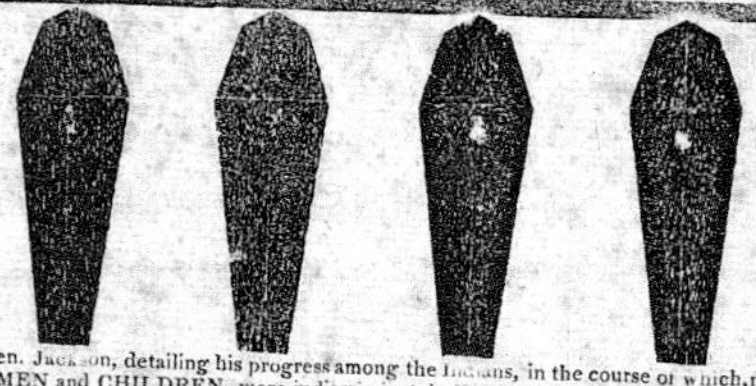

Gen. Jackson, detailing his progress among the Indians, in the course of which, men, WOMEN and CHILDREN, were indiscriminately "exterminated," their towns burnt and their country laid waste, with the utmost complacency and *sang froid*, says, in his letter dated, "Camp before St. Marks, April 9, 1818"—"Capt. M'Ever having hoisted English colours on board of his boats, Francis *the Prophet*, Hocomochemutcho and *two others*, were *decoyed* on board. *These have been hung to-day!*" Reader, mark the perfect indifference with which Gen. Jackson shoots, hangs or stabs his fellow beings, with or without trial, and the more than callous, aye, even exulting composure, with which he details his horrid and bloody deeds! If the Indians, according to the customs of their nation, put to death a prisoner, all the feelings of our nature rise into indignation against them. With what feelings then should we contemplate the *decoying* and cold-blooded murder of prisoners, by a civilized man, in the face of the laws and customs of his country!

FRANKLIN, Tenn. September 10, 1818.

A difference which had been for some months brewing between Gen. Jackson and myself, produced on Saturday, he 4th inst. in the town of Nashville, the most outrageous affray ever witnessed in a civilized country. In communicating the affair to my friends and fellow-citizens, I limit myself to the statement of a few leading facts, the truth of which I am ready to establish by judicial proofs.

1. That myself and my brother, Jesse Benton, arriving in Nashville on the morning of the affray, and knowing of General Jackson's threats, went and took lodgings in a different house from the one in which he staid, on purpose to avoid him.

2. That the General and some of his friends came the house where we had put up, and commenced the attack by levelling a pistol at me, when I had no weapon drawn, and advancing upon me at a quick pace, without giving me time to draw one.

3. That seeing this, my brother fired upon General Jackson, when he had got within eight or ten feet of me.

4. That four other pistols were fired in quick succession; one by General Jackson at me; two by me at the General; and one by Col. Coffee at me. In the course of this firing, General Jackson was brought to the ground; but received no hurt.

5. That daggers were then drawn. Col. Coffee and Mr. Alexander Donaldson made at me, and gave me five slight wounds. Captain Hammond and Mr. Stokeley Hays engaged my brother, who being still weak from the effect of a severe wound he had lately received in a duel, was not able to resist two men. They got him down; and while Capt. Hammond beat him on the head to make him lie still, Mr. Hays attempted to stab him, and wounded him in both arms, as he lay on his back parrying the thrusts with his naked hands. From this situation a generous hearted citizen of Nashville, Mr. Summer, relieved him. Before he came to the ground, my brother clapped a pistol to the breast of Mr. Hays, to blow him through, but it missed fire.

6. My own and my brother's pistols carried two balls each; for it was our intention, if driven to arms, to have no child's play. The pistols fired at me were so near that the blaze of the muzzle of one of them burnt the sleeve of my coat, and the other aimed at my head at a little more than arms length from it.

7. Capt. Carroll was to have taken part in the affray, but was absent by the permission of General Jackson, as he has proved by the General's certificate, a certificate which reflects I know not whether less honor upon the General or upon the Captain.

8. That this attack was made upon me in the house where the Judge of the District, Mr. Searcy, had his lodgings! Nor has the civil authority yet taken cognizance of this horrible outrage.

These facts are sufficient to fix the public opinion. For my own part, I think it scandalous that such things should take place at any time; but particularly so at the present moment, when the public service requires the aid of all its citizens.—As for the name of *courage*, God forbid that I should ever attempt to gain it by becoming a bully.—Those who know me, know full well that I would give a thousand times more for the reputation of Croghan in defending his post, than I would for the reputation of all the duellists and gladiators that ever appeared upon the face of the earth.

THOMAS HART BENTON, *Lieut. Col. 39th Infantry.*

And now a member of the Senate of the United States

Oklahoma Colony!

A Colony has been organized for the purpose of opening up and settling this beautiful country lying south of the State of Kansas. This Colony will start for that country on June 25, 1883, and will settle upon and occupy this famous and fertile country. This is the last and only chance to secure for yourselves homes upon government lands that have heretofore been held for the Indians. This country belongs to the government and is surveyed and sectionized. Capt. D. L. Payne, the famous Oklahoma agitator, will lecture upon this subject

TO·NIGHT!

fully relating the progress made by previous expeditions to that country, and will give his hearers a truthful description of the country and the present status of the colony.

Every person who desires to secure an excellent home, should not fail to attend the lecture.

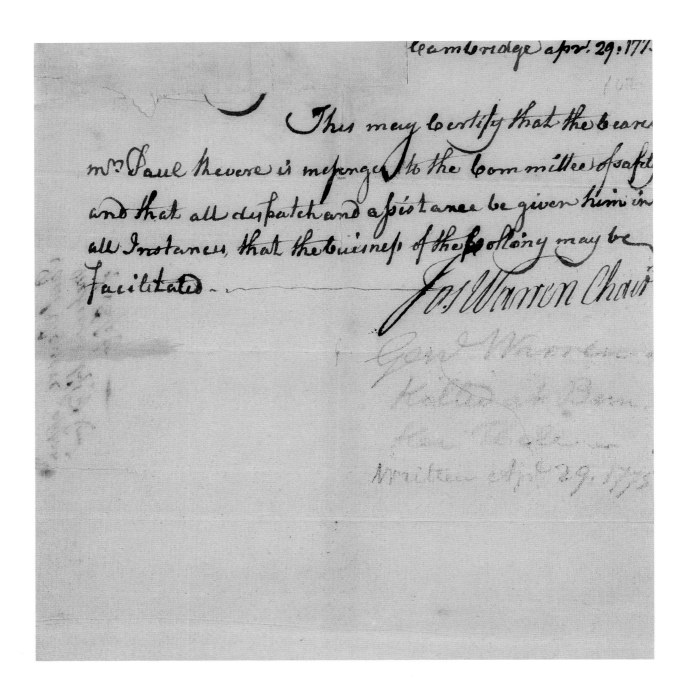

This document, really just a note, was written only eleven days after Paul Revere's now famous ride. At this time Joseph Warren, its author, was chairman of the colony's Committee of Safety and the most powerful person in Massachusetts. A Committee of Safety carried on responsibilities of the government within a colony prior to and during the early years of the American Revolution. Its members usually represented the revolutionary leadership and were appointed by the colonial assembly. At the beginning of the war they were frequently the only governing body in existence. As stability returned, the committees gradually gave way to state constitutions, with executives and legislatures. Dr. Joseph Warren, who also held the presidency of the Massachusetts legislature, soon succeeded John Hancock. Warren distinguished himself as a student at Harvard, married well, and was soon known as an excellent physician. By 1765 he was becoming far more active in politics than in his medical practice. He assumed numerous public duties and became active in the political clubs of the day. At town meetings he often appeared with Samuel Adams, John Hancock, and James Otis. In response to the approaching crisis he decided to abandon his profession and to enter the army.

As Chairman of the Committee of Safety, Warren selected Paul Revere to recruit volunteers and locate provisions in preparation for the siege of Boston. This note from Warren provided the authority Revere needed to carry out his charge. During the siege in June 1775, Warren was killed in the final assault on Breed's Hill. A British commander later wrote the he "stuffed the scoundrel with another rebel into one hole, and there he and his seditious principles may remain." Paul Revere and two of Warren's brothers later recovered the body. Warren was remembered as "burning with intense patriotism." His death was mourned as a national calamity and, according to Daniel Webster, Warren became "the first great martyr to this great cause." Paul Revere named his next-born son Joseph Warren Revere.

THOMAS JEFFERSON wrote this letter to William Fleming on July 1, 1776—only three days before his draft of the Declaration of Independence was formally adopted by the Continental Congress in Philadelphia. Jefferson mentioned numerous events relating to the war effort, the need for "hard money with which to procure provisions . . . the ravages of small pox with which one half of our army is still down . . . the unlucky choice of some officers . . . ."

In the final paragraph of the letter Jefferson expressed concern over the decreased number of votes he received in a recent election of Virginia delegates to the Continental Congress. "It is a painful situation to be 300 miles from one's country, and thereby open to secret assassination without a possibility of self-defense. . . . If any doubt has arisen as to me, my country will have my political creed in the form of a 'Declaration etc.' which I was lately directed to draw. This will give decisive proof that my own sentiment concurred with the vote they instructed us to give."

Jefferson's mention of a Declaration is in reference to the resolution that called for complete American independence. Early in June, the Continental Congress appointed a committee to draft a statement declaring the reasons for the impending separation of the colonies from Great Britain. Jefferson (only thirty-three at the time) was not a highly visible member of Congress, although outspoken and decisive in committees. It was a splendid but dangerous opportunity for a man who had the reputation of a masterly pen. He prepared the draft, submitting it to the committee for consideration. John Adams and Benjamin Franklin suggested minor changes, but the final words were still largely those of Jefferson.

William Fleming (1729-1795) was a soldier and statesman who immigrated to Virginia from Scotland in 1755. Known for his dignity, courtesy, and intellect, he was a longstanding friend of Jefferson.

+

THOMAS JEFFERSON American, 1743-1826
LETTER TO WILLIAM FLEMING, 1776
3826.71

DRAFTED BY THOMAS JEFFERSON between June 11 and
June 28, 1778, the Declaration of Independence is one of the
most important documents in the history of the United
States. The political philosophy of the Declaration was not
new; John Locke and others had expressed its ideals of
individual liberty. Jefferson summarized this philosophy of
"self-evident truths" and set forth a list of grievances against
the King of England in order to justify before the world the
breaking of ties between the American colonies and the
mother country.

After the formal declaration of the colonies'
independence and throughout the Revolutionary War, the
new American nation sought recognition and support from
the kingdoms of Europe. To this end Benjamin Franklin, Silas
Deane, and Arthur Lee served as American commissioners
plenipotentiary. Headquartered in Paris and acting on
instructions of the Continental Congress, they sent a letter
along with the certified copies of the Declaration of

Independence and the Articles of Confederation to Baron de
Schulenburg, minister to Frederick the Great of Prussia.
Their aim was to promote friendship and commerce with the
newly formed United States. Prussia did not assist the
American cause directly. Frederick, however, refused to side
with the British and thus added to Great Britain's isolation in
the European community.

This is the only official certified copy of the Declaration
of Independence known to have survived to the present. It is
Franklin's and Deane's signatures that constitute the
certification. The document was included in 1948 on the
Freedom Train, the American Heritage Foundation's project
to display great documents of history throughout the country.
Gilcrease purchased it through the rare book dealer Philip
Rosenbach in 1950, along with the certified copy of the
Articles of Confederation, Franklin and Deane's letter to
Baron de Schulenburg, and the latter's response, which is
written in French. All are now at Gilcrease Museum.

+

DECLARATION OF INDEPENDENCE, 1777

4026.901

Quicapú.

Kickapoos: Indigènes originaires des frontières du Canada, emigrés dans le
Nord du Texas.

Jean Louis Berlandier was a Swiss-trained botanist who traveled as a member of the Mexican Comisión de Límits (Boundary Commission). Formed to determine the border between Mexico and the United States in the region of the Sabine and Red Rivers, the expedition left Mexico City in November of 1827 and traveled in northern Mexico and southern Texas during 1828-29. Under the leadership of General Manuel Mier y Terán (1789-1832), the Comisión collected information on the geography, natural resources, soils, minerals, and plant and animal life in the border region. It was also responsible for recording data on the dispositions, customs, and attitudes of the native peoples and of the Americans who were beginning to populate the area. Watercolors, including this one, were created as part of the expedition. Many are designated as having been painted following original sketches by Lieutenant José María Sánchez y Tapia (the artist-cartographer of the expedition who died in 1834) or by Jean Louis Berlandier.

This watercolor was painted by Lino Sánchez y Tapia,

although he noted on the work that Lt. Sánchez prepared the original drawing. Stylistically it is akin to the work of a group of Mexican artists labeled the Costumbristas who painted regional, ethnic, and class costume in a manner fashionable in Mexico since its introduction in 1825. It is probable that the subject is one of two Kickapoo deer hunters that Lt. Sánchez and General Terán met along the Trinity River east of Nacogdoches in May of 1828. Sánchez recorded the encounter in his diary, writing, "I noticed that their appearance is more fierce than that of other Indians, revealing in their manners a certain pride which is their characteristic." However, as with all thirty-nine watercolors in this volume, the setting is conventionalized and the figure not intended as a portrait; rather, emphasis is on clothing and accessories typical of the tribe depicted. Original versions of Berlandier's journals are at the Gilcrease Museum, the Library of Congress, and the Western Americana Collection at Yale University. The Gilcrease volumes include the set of thirty-nine watercolors by Lino Sánchez y Tapia.

+

LINO SÁNCHEZ Y TAPIA Mexican, ?-1838
QUICAPÚ, ca. 1834
4016.336

SE-QUO-YAH.

Philadelphia Published by F. C. Biddle

SEQUOYAH (C. 1770S-1843) was the only American Indian north of Mexico to invent a method of expressing a native language in written form. His writing system, perfected and made public about 1821, offered a new means of communication to the Cherokee people. Often referred to as the Sequoyan syllabary, it includes symbols that each represent a syllable in the Cherokee language.

There remains much controversy concerning the life and work of Sequoyah. His native name was Sikwayi, which became Sequoyah to non-Cherokee speakers; he was also known as George Gist or George Guess. His father, a British merchant and later an American soldier, was absent from Sequoyah's life. He grew up in the care of his mother, in eastern Tennessee, surrounded by Cherokees following traditional beliefs. Sequoyah became a metal craftsman and was respected for mechanical and inventive abilities. Perhaps as early as 1809, he became interested in the concept of a written language and began to experiment with designing a pictograph for every word. Gradually this concept was refined, and he divided the Cherokee language into eighty-six syllables. He faced ridicule and accusations of trafficking in witchcraft to uncover a secret such as writing, but through his invention he hoped to preserve Cherokee culture and

religion. Sequoyah's invention was so phonetically accurate that native speakers could master the written language in only a few days. Within months thousands could read and write in their own language. With modifications to allow for capitalization, punctuation, and other conventions, the syllabary was reproduced in moveable type, making it possible to print the *Cherokee Advocate* newspaper and other documents. In 1824 the Cherokee Nation had a medal struck in Sequoyah's honor. A bronze of Sequoyah is displayed at Statuary Hall at the Capitol in Washington, D.C., and his portrait is in the Oklahoma State Capitol building. In 1847 the giant redwood trees of California were named *sequoia gigantean* in his honor.

The hand-colored lithograph of Sequoyah shown above is after an 1828 portrait by Charles Bird King. The original painting, commissioned by Thomas McKenney and James Hall for *History of the Indian Tribes of North America,* burned in the Smithsonian fire of 1865.

The document on the facing page, written by Sequoyah, includes the numbering system he developed and the syllabary. The syllabary (the lower three lines) is followed by Sequoyah's signature in the lower right corner.

+

SEQUOYAH Cherokee, c. 1770S-1843
SYLLABARY
4026.312

Heads of Families	Males Over 10	Females Over 10	Males under 10	Females under 10	Slaves Over 10	Slaves under 10	Total	Wagons	Horses	Oxen	Colts
Robert	1	1	1	2	"	"	5	"	"	"	"
Lightning Bug	1	1	2	1	"	"	5	"	1	"	"
Nah hoo la	2	2	2	2	"	"	8	"	1	"	"
Oo la yo oh	1	"	"	"	"	"	1	"	"	"	"
Naw Ke	"	1	"	"	"	"	1	"	"	"	"
Oo da yo soo	1	1	"	"	"	"	2	"	1	"	"
Chewaloohee	1	1	"	"	"	"	2	"	"	"	"
Tal yoo leeskee	1	1	1	"	"	"	3	"	"	"	"
Sa te gah	1	1	"	"	"	"	2	"	"	"	"
Thomas	1	2	"	1	"	"	4	"	1	"	"
Jacksaw too wago	1	1	1	"	"	"	3	"	"	"	"
Tse too wau no	1	1	1	2	"	"	5	"	1	"	"
Will Scott	1	2	1	"	"	"	4	"	2	"	2
Yda da che	1	3	"	"	"	"	4	"	1	"	"
Sa chun Sey	1	3	1	"	"	"	5	"	1	"	1
Qualy	"	1	4	"	"	"	5	"	2	"	1
Yo too wo ta	1	2	"	1	"	"	4	"	4	"	1
Yo noo gas kee	1	"	"	"	"	"	1	"	"	"	"
A ne cha	1	1	"	"	"	"	2	"	1	"	"
Cul stee	"	1	"	"	"	"	1	"	"	"	"
Cun no ta te	1	"	"	"	"	"	1	"	"	"	"
Da la nos ta	1	"	"	"	"	"	1	"	"	"	"
Tom too wau go	1	"	"	"	"	"	1	"	"	"	"
Wilson too wau go	3	2	"	1	"	"	6	"	3	"	"
Moses too wau go	1	1	"	"	"	"	2	"	1	"	"
Betsey	"	2	1	2	"	"	5	"	1	"	"
Crying Turkey	1	"	"	"	"	"	1	"	"	"	"
John Davis	1	"	"	"	"	"	1	"	"	"	"

CHIEF JOHN ROSS (1790–1866) served the Cherokee tribe for over fifty years, proving himself an exceptional chief executive, political negotiator, and diplomat. Of mixed Scottish and Cherokee ancestry, he was raised in a family that believed in education and took pride in its Cherokee heritage. In 1827 Ross became involved in one of the landmark events of Cherokee history. He was elected a delegate to the convention that created the first constitutional government of an American Indian tribe; later he would become the group's president. The following year the General Council elected Ross the first chief under the new constitution. For the next ten years Ross and the Cherokees resisted pressure from the state of Georgia and the federal government to remove the people from their traditional homelands. But by the mid-1830s tribal solidarity waned as a minority began to believe that survival depended upon moving West, beyond white influence. This minority signed the Treaty of New Echota.

Ross campaigned untiringly to overturn the treaty, which provided for total removal to western lands, but by July 1838, General Winfield Scott's troops had moved most of the tribe into confinement camps in preparation for removal. Ross was appointed by the General Council, with the approval of the federal government, to take over as removal superintendent. The Cherokee Nation was organized into thirteen detachments of about 1,000 persons each. Every detachment

included conductors, physicians, interpreters, commissary agents, and wagon masters. On the 800-mile journey the detachments encountered drought, bitter winter weather, constant sickness, exposure to the elements, and corruption of those hired to furnish provisions. The removal process resulted in the deaths of more than 4,000 Cherokee people.

James D. Wofford and Chuwalookee [Chooalooka] were leaders of one of the Cherokee detachments. This muster roll includes listings for heads of families with men, women, slaves, wagons, and livestock in each group. The photograph of John Ross shown here was taken in Philadelphia in 1863. Ross spent most of the Civil War years in Washington and Philadelphia working to convince the Lincoln administration that the Cherokees were coerced into supporting the Confederacy.

JOHN ROSS PAPERS — MUSTER ROLL, 1838

4026.8435

KARL BODMER (1809–1893) was a young and little-known Swiss artist when he was employed by German Prince Maximilian to record his travel among the native peoples of the northern American Plains from 1832–1834. In preparation for their western travels, the royal ethnologist and his artist examined museums and libraries in Boston and Philadelphia, visited some of America's leading scientific men in the utopian colony of New Harmony, Indiana, and then traveled on toward the largely uncharted Plains and Rocky Mountains. Leaving St. Louis on an American Fur Company steamboat and later transferring to keelboats, Prince Maximilian's expedition visited a series of forts. The westernmost point of their journey was Fort Mackenzie in what is now central Montana.

Upon his return to Europe, Maximilian began the process of editing his extensive journals for publication. Between 1839 and 1843 German, French, and English editions of his text were published. A picture atlas of hand-colored aquatint engravings based upon Bodmer's watercolors accompanied the narrative. The plates, which were printed in Paris under the artist's supervision, have trilingual captions. The publication provided some of the earliest accurate descriptions of many Plains tribes to reach the general public. Of Bodmer's hundreds of watercolors and drawings, eighty-one were finally reproduced as aquatint engravings.

The Gilcrease Museum collection includes Maximilian's text in German and English as well as the accompanying picture atlas. There are also two early versions of the aquatint plate *Interior of the Hut of a Mandan Chief*. In addition, there is an original sepia wash of the same image.

While wintering at Fort Clark, Maximilian's expedition frequently visited the Mandan winter village Mih-Tutta-Hang-Kusch. The Mandan lodge interior that Bodmer depicted was the home of Dipäuch, a respected elder who provided much information about the history and beliefs of the tribe. *Interior of the Hut of a Mandan Chief*, sketched over a four-month span, is an excellent example of the artist's careful depiction of detail. The accouterments of a warrior are prominent, as are the heavy supporting pillars and roof beams. The materials of daily life—cooking jars, hand pouches, and utensils—are also visible. This image reveals the appearance of the plate before the application of color.

+

Journal, &c. Continued.

Santa Fé, Feb. 25, 1840. — Having adjusted my business in Santa Fé, our waggons left to day for the U. S. with intention of returning down the Rio Colorado, or Canadian Fork of Arkansas, — in the vicinity of the route we came, although we will no doubt frequently be at some distance from our former trail, as we will endeavour to straighten the route.

I brought from Chihuahua 21 waggons added to 6 remaining in Santa Fé, make 27, and one belonging to Messrs. Wethered and Ware Completes our Caravan of 28 waggons, and upwards of 200 mules. — Our Company, besides myself, and William Baxter, Consists of Joseph N. Dornstein, out-riders — Benj. Hambright, Jesse Amick, James Revoldy, * Also Henry Trell, Tailor, (not hired.)

Josiah Gregg (1806–1850) is remembered as a literary historian and a chronicler of life and trade on the Santa Fe Trail in the 1830s. Gregg first journeyed across the Southern Plains in 1831 in search of relief from failing health. The rigors of travel, the austere diet, and the different climate provided a revitalizing change; within a few months into his journey Gregg was a healthy man. During the next nine years Gregg made the arduous journey to Santa Fe eight times. He soon became a trader, establishing a base in Santa Fe and later traveling on to Saltillo and Chihuahua, Mexico. The Santa Fe trade, which had flourished as merchants from the United States transported goods to the northern provinces of Mexico, began to decline in the late 1830s. The trade was closed by the Mexican government in 1843 because of border disagreements with the Republic of Texas. The United States government supported the Texans on a number of issues and tensions increased with the Mexicans.

A devoted observer of life on the western frontier, Gregg maintained extensive journals throughout his expeditions. From these writings he published *Commerce of the Prairies* in 1844. The two-volume set was well received by critics and the general public. The work was acclaimed for its support of the expansionist policies of the United States and of the doctrine of Manifest Destiny. By the conclusion of the Mexican War and the surrender of the territory of New Mexico to the United States in 1850, a fifth edition had been printed. *Commerce of the Prairies* contains a mix of chapters devoted to the author's adventures and to his scientific observations. Gregg wrote of the hardships of travel, the excitement of buffalo hunts, and the conflicts with Native Americans. His scientific observations contained commentary on the natural history of the Southern Plains and descriptions of the landscape. His measurements of routes, distances, and waterways allowed for the creation of maps of New Mexico that were used for years.

Gregg's writing reflects the cultural biases common in the mid 19th century in the United States. His bias is evident in his criticism of several Native American tribes, of Catholic Hispanics, and of Mormons. Even considering these flaws, Gregg's writing surpasses that of many of his contemporaries through a prose style that conveys a sense of authenticity without the fashionable embellishments. He did not view his work as having political or concealed meanings; he considered his writing an outgrowth of his "passion for Prairie life."

+

JOSIAH GREGG American, 1806–1850
PAGE FROM THE JOURNAL OF JOSIAH GREGG, FEBRUARY 1840
TITLE PAGE FROM COMMERCE OF THE PRAIRIES
3616.211 (title page), 4326.5964, 2526.1451

COMMERCE OF THE PRAIRIES:

OR THE

𝔍𝔬𝔲𝔯𝔫𝔞𝔩 𝔬𝔣 𝔞 𝔖𝔞𝔫𝔱𝔞 𝔉é 𝔗𝔯𝔞𝔡𝔢𝔯,

DURING

EIGHT EXPEDITIONS ACROSS

THE GREAT WESTERN PRAIRIES,

AND

A RESIDENCE OF NEARLY NINE YEARS

IN

NORTHERN MEXICO.

Illustrated with Maps and Engravings.

BY JOSIAH GREGG.

IN TWO VOLUMES.

VOL. I.

NEW YORK:

HENRY G. LANGLEY, 8 ASTOR HOUSE.

———

M DCCC XLIV.

GEORGE CATLIN—artist, explorer, promoter—is well examined in the art history of the American West. Within the Gilcrease Museum collection of Catlin works is a truly remarkable item entitled *Souvenir of the North American Indians as they were, in the middle of the Nineteenth Century*. This bound volume contains 100 pages, fifty exquisite watercolors each with a facing page of text in Catlin's hand. The title page is signed by Catlin and dated *Egyptian Hall, London, 1849*.

The watercolor plates are based on paintings from Catlin's "Indian Gallery," a body of works inspired by his travels in North America during the 1830s. Approximately the first half of the volume contains depictions of individuals, often in groups of three. The second half includes hunting and dance scenes. Catlin's narrative is also appealing. His subjects are not unknown stereotypical people and events. Catlin writes that this is Ba∕da∕ah∕chon∕du, a member of the Crow tribe, who modeled most of a day for the painting. The watercolor presents finely crafted details of the feathered bonnets of both the horse and rider. The quillwork strips on the shirt and leggings of the rider are also delicately executed.

The *Souvenir of the North American Indians* was offered for sale to the British bibliophile and collector, Sir Thomas Phillipps. In a letter dated February 21, 1858 (also in the Gilcrease collection) Catlin states, "And, as I am always disposed to give Sir Thomas Phillipps the first chance, I send herewith another epitome of my collection, made a long time ago. They were formerly bound up in the canvas which are now loose upon them, and which I cut off, in order to give a double thickness to the paper on which the drawings are mounted." Phillipps did decide to purchase the group and evidently had it bound. Thomas Gilcrease acquired the volume from the Phillipps estate in 1947.

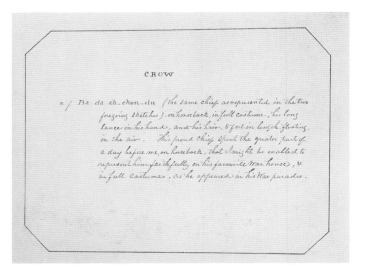

+

JOHN GOULD (1804-1881) was a British ornithologist whose fifty-year career included publications on birds of the Himalayan Mountains, Europe, Australia, Asia, and Great Britain. His volumes on hummingbirds, *The Monograph of Trochilidae*, published between 1849 and 1861, are possibly the most beautiful of all his work. Like many of his time, Gould was fascinated by the tiny birds sometimes called "flying jewels." His interest developed into a multi-volume publication with 418 hand-colored plates depicting hummingbirds with appropriate flowers.

Gould first worked as a taxidermist, an important field in 19th-century England where skins of exotic creatures constantly arrived for scientific study or for use as home decoration. He did not see living hummingbirds until 1857 on a trip to the United States. In his London home, Gould's collection of mounted specimens grew to include more than 300 species. Most of the collection was sold to the British Museum following his death. During Gould's time, millions of hummingbirds were exported to Europe, primarily from South America and the West Indies. One London dealer reportedly imported more than 400,000 in a single year. The skins were fashioned into jewelry such as pins and brooches. Although involved in the collection of birds for scientific research, Gould spoke out against the use of feathers for hats and other fashionable adornments.

Hummingbirds are found only in the Western Hemisphere, the greatest number of species in South America. Their luminosity and apparent brilliant color is produced by diffraction and reflection of light through the microscopic structure of their feathers. Here Gould has depicted the nest of a *Clytolaema Rubinea* of southern Brazil, which, he noted, was found among the branches of the loftiest trees of the forest. The nests are delicate cups made of fine animal and plant down, mosses, and lichens held together with spider silk and the bird's saliva. The eggs, usually a pair, hatch in twelve to nineteen days.

+

JOHN GOULD British, 1804-1882
THE MONOGRAPH OF TROCHILIDAE, PART 6, PLATE 2
3276.52

Esa-to-yetz - Commanch Chief

PHOTOGRAPHY, a process combining science and art, was first made public in 1839. The relatively inexpensive process quickly seized the public imagination, producing an almost immediate demand for portraits. In America, photography moved from the studio to the field during the Civil War. And in the postwar era the Western frontier emerged as a rich resource for scenic and scientific exploration photography.

William S. Soule (1836-1908) served as a photographer with the Union Army during the American Civil War. In 1867 he traveled to Fort Dodge, Kansas. The following year he moved to Camp Supply and then to Fort Sill in Indian Territory. With the unique opportunity of time and location, he served as post photographer at the recently built fort. Soule captured images of members of the Cheyenne, Comanche, and Kiowa tribes during a difficult time of transition. Soule is best known for his photographs of Plains peoples, although he remained in the West only seven years.

+

WILLIAM S. SOULE American, 1836-1908
ESA-TO-YETA, COMANCHE CHIEF
Photograph, 4516.90.9

TOWER FALLS

WILLIAM HENRY JACKSON (1843–1942) was one of the most famous and most prolific of 19th-century western photographers. Between 1870 and 1879 he served as the photographer of the Hayden United States Geological Survey, becoming the first to photograph what would become Yellowstone National Park. During the 1880s and 1890s he maintained a studio in Denver while photographing extensively the landscape and people of the American West and Mexico. He later traveled throughout the world as the photographer for the World Transportation Commission.

✢

WILLIAM HENRY JACKSON American, 1843–1942
TOWER FALLS
Photograph, 4536.84.17

A Typical Boomer Family.

WILLIAM S. PRETTYMAN (1858-1932) arrived in Kansas in 1879, became a photographer's apprentice, and soon opened his own studio. He first photographed many native peoples in his studio and beginning in 1883 traveled extensively through Indian Territory. Prettyman also recorded land openings in the area and the founding of towns such as Guthrie and Oklahoma City.

＋

WILLIAM S. PRETTYMAN American, 1858-1932
A TYPICAL BOOMER FAMILY
Photograph, 4527.85.17

Edward S. Curtis (1868–1952) worked to record the lifestyles of native peoples in America. Between 1907 and 1930 he published *The North American Indian*, twenty volumes and twenty portfolios together containing more than 3,500 photogravures. Depicted are the daily life, ceremonies, and customs of more than eighty tribes. Considered a romantic, he often retouched negatives and printed them with a soft tone to eliminate background details and create a dramatic mood.

+

EDWARD S. CURTIS American, 1868–1952
THE RUSH GATHERER–KUTENAI
THE NORTH AMERICAN INDIAN PORTFOLIO 7, PLATE 255
Photogravure, 4327.970.36

THE EARLY ART OF NATIVE PEOPLES OF THE AMERICAS was a form of religious expression, a depiction of tribal history, and a personal narrative. Throughout the Western Plains, men recorded scenes or events on animal hides. In the late 19th century, with the availability of new materials, an amazing explosion of art occurred. The new materials included plain accounting books, along with pens, pencils, colored pencils, and crayons, obtained as gifts, through trade, or from raids. One resulting tradition became known as Plains ledger drawing because the works were executed on ruled ledgers. Ledger drawings were most often narrative in form, recounting events worthy of remembrance.

Ledger art is a unique Native American artistic expression and is highly stylized and sophisticated. Its distinctive stylistic traits are marked by a composition that progresses from right to left. There is no attempt to create an impression of background and no illusion of depth or shadowing. Figures are portrayed in abstract form rather than photographic proportion, and heads are shown in profile. An artist began by creating outlines or contours, which were then filled in with color. The highly detailed designs of clothing, accoutrements, or face paint distinguish particular individuals.

+

FORT RENO LEDGER BOOK ARTIST
COURTING SCENE, CA. 1887

4526.11.40

The LEDGER BOOK from which this drawing and the one on the facing page were taken was created by the Cheyenne scouts at Fort Reno, Indian Territory, and inscribed *1887*. Scouts were recruited from the Southern Cheyenne and Arapaho reservations in 1885 to serve at Fort Reno, which was near the Darlington agency in the west central part of what would become the state of Oklahoma. Seventy men joined Scout Company A of the 22nd Infantry, which was not disbanded until 1895. Terms of service were for six-month periods, and most men reenlisted as each term was completed. Inscriptions indicate that the ledger was, at least for a time, in the possession of Neal W. Evans, who owned a trading post at Fort Reno from the 1870s until the 1890s.

Additional inscriptions identify an artist or subject depicted in the ledger book. The volume contains 140 images, twenty-four with names, which were drawn by at least eight artists.

The central figure in this drawing of a Cheyenne warrior is probably Red Eagle, seen counting coup on an enemy. The warrior is identified by his personal shield and headdress. He also carries a military society quirt.

The drawing on the facing page depicts a courting scene. Courting may be clearly shown or simply implied. Men and women may appear together in a variety of situations. Women are also depicted in activities such as traveling or cooking.

+

FORT RENO LEDGER BOOK ARTIST
COUNTING COUP, CA. 1887
4526.11.96

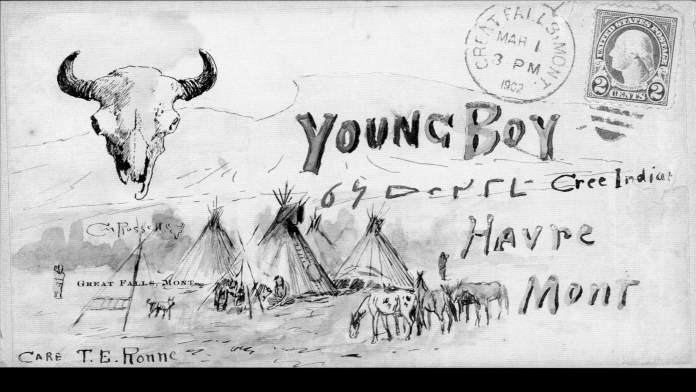

IN MARCH 1902 Charles M. Russell wrote to Young Boy, a Cree he had known since the mid 1890s. He conveyed his thanks to Young Boy for the shield depicted in the letter and for some pictures also sent, and wrote, "I will paint your picture as soon as I can." Young Boy was a member of a group known as the Canadian Cree who faced extreme hardships until a small reservation was created for them in 1916 near Havre, Montana. Through the years, Russell hired Young Boy for many odd jobs, including modeling. Russell's illustrated envelope and letter did not depict the harsh present, but the better times of the past.

Charles Russell, a preeminent artist of the Old West, was born in St. Louis but Montana was his chosen home. Much of his art sought to recreate a vanished past, nostalgically recalled. Besides paintings and sculpture, Russell's career included illustrations for magazines and books, among them volumes by Theodore Roosevelt, Bret Harte, and Owen Wister. He also wrote his own first-person stories of western life and illustrated letters. Writing—inscriptions, poems, letters, or published stories—was not easy for Russell. He eventually began to use images to express himself on paper.

This he termed "paper talk." In this mode, rules of grammar, spelling, and punctuation did not apply. In 1929, three years after her husband's death, Nancy Russell published 145 of Charlie Russell's illustrated letters in a volume entitled *Good Medicine*, so titled, she said, "because they bring a kindly thought or laugh." *Good Medicine* was an immediate favorite with Russell admirers.

Russell's final illustrated letter was written to Philip Cole. It was included in *Good Medicine*. In the table of contents of the volume Nancy Russell identified Philip G. Cole as "A native Montanan. Physician. Owner of the largest individual collection of Russell paintings." Cole greatly desired to receive one of Russell's famous illustrated letters. In response to Cole's often-repeated request, Russell wrote his last illustrated letter to him, dated just a month before the artist's death. Russell thanks Cole for a gift of Will James's books, explains that the elk sketched at the top of the letter was a small band seen near the Russell's mountain camp, and hopes that it will remind Cole of the country from which he comes.

and when it coms to makeing the beautiful
Ma nature has man beat all ways from
the ace
and that old lady still owns a lot of
montana
to show what I mean man made this
animal takina but the old lady Im
about made this one
I have made a living painting
pictures of the horned on and
the life about him it took regular men
to handle real cows
I would starve to drath painting the hornles
deformity
God made cows with hornes to defend herself
and when a wolf got meat it wasent easy
often he was so full of horn holes he wasent
hungry a weasel could kill the man one with out
getting a serach
but I forgot Iv got no kick coming Iv
been trimed my self
but the medicine men at Rochester
onely took from me things I dident need
and was glad to get rid of
I look and feel better but Im still very
weak
if you see Olaf Seltzer give him my
regards
I suppose by this time hes a real Newyorker
we have been having lots of snow but to day
it has cleard and I think the storm is over
we all send our best regards to you and
yours
Your friend
C M Russell

ALEXANDER POSEY (1873–1908) was a poet, politician, journalist, and political satirist. He was the first Native American to achieve national recognition as a poet, a distinction repeated when he became the owner and editor of a daily newspaper, the *Indian Journal* in Eufaula, Creek Nation.

Posey began writing while attending Bacone College in the early 1890s. He eventually penned more than 250 poems, with works appearing in numerous area newspapers in 1899 and 1900. Despite acclamation for his poetry, Posey turned to political satire. Writing in the persona of Fus Fixico and in dialect—Posey discussed politics in the Creek Nation, the dissolution of tribal lands, approaching statehood, fraud committed by public officials, and the difficulties of some native people in adjusting to changes in their society.

In addition to his literary endeavors, Posey was involved in politics. He was elected to the Creek National Council when he was only twenty-two, held several government posts (including superintendent of schools for the Creek Nation),

and worked for the Dawes Commission enrolling Creeks for land allotments. Posey lived during a complex time of cultural transition, and his progressive views often placed him at odds with more traditional Creek beliefs. But his ethnic ambivalence—along with his charisma, intellect, humor, and leadership skills—gave Posey a powerful voice within the tribe. Alexander Posey's poetry reflected his affection for the people and landscapes of his homeland, while his satire illuminated and documented conditions within Indian Territory.

A transcription of this hand-written poem reads:

Fancy

Why do trees along the river
 Lean so far out o'er the tide?
Cold reason tells me why, but
 I am never satisfied.

And so I keep my fancy still
 That trees lean out to save
The drowning from the clutches of
 The cold remorseless wave.

+

Archuleta, Margaret, and Dr. Rennard Strickland. *Shared Visions: Native American Painting and Sculpture in the Twentieth Century.* New York: The New Press, 1991.

Benson, Elizabeth P., ed. *The Olmec and Their Neighbors.* Washington, DC: Dumbarton Oaks Research Library and Collections, 1981.

Berlo, Janet C. and Ruth B. Phillips. *Native North American Art.* Oxford: Oxford University Press, 1998.

Berlo, Janet Catherine, ed. *Plains Indians Drawings, 1865-1935, Pages From a Visual History.* New York: Harry N. Abrams, Inc., 1996.

Berrin, Kathleen, ed. *Art of the Huichol Indians.* New York: Harry N. Abrams, 1979.

Bradley, Douglas E. *White Swan: Crow Warrior and Painter.* Notre Dame: The Snite Museum of Art; University of Notre Dame, 1991.

Broder, Patricia Janis. *American Indian Painting and Sculpture.* New York: Abbeville Press, 1981.

Broder, Patricia Janis. *Earth Songs, Moon Dreams: Paintings by American Indian Women.* New York: St. Martin's Press, 1999.

Brody, J. J. *Indian Painters and White Patrons.* Albuquerque: University of New Mexico Press, 1971.

Buisseret, David, ed. *From Sea Charts to Satellite Images: Interpreting North American History through Maps.* Chicago: The University of Chicago Press, 1990.

Callander, Lee A., and David M. Fawcett. *Native American Painting: Selections From the Museum of the American Indian.* New York: Museum of the American Indian, 1982.

Catesby, Mark. *Catesby's Birds of Colonial America.* Chapel Hill: University of North Carolina Press, 1985.

Cordry, Donald. *Mexican Masks.* Austin: University of Texas Press, 1980.

Dippie, Brian W., ed. *Charles Russell, Word Painter: Letters, 1887-1926.* Fort Worth: Amon Carter Museum, 1993.

Dittert, Alfred E. Jr. and Fred Plogg. *Generations in Clay: Pueblo Pottery of the American Southwest.* Flagstaff: Northland Press, 1980.

Dunn, Dorothy. *American Indian Painting of the Southwest and Plains Areas.* Albuquerque: University of New Mexico Press, 1968.

Ellis, Joseph, et al. *Thomas Jefferson: Genius of Liberty.* New York: Viking Studio in association with the Library of Congress, 2000.

Esser, Janet Brody, ed. *Behind the Mask in Mexico.* Santa Fe: The Museum of New Mexico Press, 1988.

Ewers, John C., ed. *The Indians of Texas in 1830 by Jean Louis Berlandier.* Washington, D.C.: Smithsonian Institution Press, 1969.

Farnsworth, Kenneth B. and Thomas E. Emerson. "The Macoupin Creek Figure Pipe and Its Archaeological Context." *Midcontinental Journal of Archaeology* 14 (1): 18-33, 1989.

Fischer, David Hackett. *Paul Revere's Ride.* New York: Oxford University Press, 1994.

Galloway, Patricia, ed. *The Southeastern Ceremonial Complex: Artifacts and Analysis.* Lincoln: University of Nebraska Press, 1989.

Hail, Barbara A. *Hau, Kóla: The Plains Indian Collection of the Haffenreffer Museum of Anthropology.* Bristol: Haffenreffer Museum of Anthropology, 1980.

———— *Gifts of Pride and Love: Kiowa and Comanche Cradles.* Bristol: Haffenreffer Museum of Anthropology, 2000.

Highwater, Jamake. *Song From the Earth: American Indian Painting.* Boston: New York Graphic Society, 1976.

Jones, Ruthe Blalock. "Like Being Home: Oklahoma Indian Art." *Gilcrease Journal* 3.2 (1995): 6-21.

Kaufman, Alice and Christopher Selser. *The Navajo Weaving Tradition, 1650 to the Present.* New York: Penguin Books, 1985.

Kehoe, Alice B. *North American Indians: A Comprehensive Account.* Englewood Cliffs: Prentice Hall, 1992.

Kramer, Barbara. *Nampeyo and Her Pottery.* Albuquerque: University of New Mexico Press, 1996.

Lantis, Margaret. "Nunivak Eskimo." In *Volume 5, Handbook of North American Indians,* ed. by David Damas, 209-223. Washington: Smithsonian Institution, 1984.

Lester, Patrick D. *The Biographical Directory of Native American Painters.* Tulsa: SIR Publications, 1995.

Littlefield, Daniel F., Jr. *Alex Posey–Creek Poet, Journalist & Humorist.* Lincoln: University of Nebraska Press, 1992.

Lothrop, S.K., W. F. Foshag and Joy Mahler. *Pre-Columbian Art.* London: Phaidon Publishers, Inc., 1957.

MacCurdy, George Grant. "A Study of Chiriquian Antiquities." In *Memoirs of the Connecticut Academy of Art and Sciences, Volume 3*. New Haven: Yale University Press, 1980.

Matuz, Roger, ed. *St. James Guide to Native North American Artists*. Detroit: St. James Press, 1998.

McLoughlin, William G. *Cherokee Renascence in the New Republic*. Princeton, NJ: Princeton University Press, 1986.

Milanich, Jerald T. and Susan Milbrath, ed. *First Encounters: Spanish Exploration of the Caribbean and United States, 1494-1570*. Gainesville: University of Florida Press, 1989.

Nelson, Edward William. "Eskimo About Bering Strait." In *Annual Report of the Bureau of American Ethnology, Volume 18, Part 1*. Washington: US Government Printing Office, 1899.

O'Connor, Mallory McCane. *Lost Cities of the Ancient Southeast*. Gainesville: University Press of Florida, 1995.

Pauketat, Timothy R and Thomas E. Emerson, eds. *Cahokia: Domination and Ideology in the Mississippian World*. Lincoln: University of Nebraska Press, 1997.

Penny, David W., ed. *Art of the American Indian Frontier*. Seattle: University of Washington Press, 1992.

Phillips, Philip and James A. Brown *Pre Columbian Shell Engravings From the Craig Mound at Spiro Oklahoma. Part 1*. Cambridge: Peabody Museum Press, 1978.

Sandweiss, Martha A., ed. *Photography in Nineteenth-Century America*. Fort Worth: Amon Carter Museum, 1991.

Sauer, Gordon C. *John Gould, The Bird Man: A Chronology and Bibliography*. Lawrence: University of Kansas Press, 1982.

Seymour, Tryntje Van Ness. *When the Rainbow Touches Down: The Artists and Stories Behind the Apache, Navajo, Rio Grande Pueblo, and Hopi Paintings in the William and Leslie Can Ness Denman Collection*. Seattle: University of Washington Press, 1988.

Silberman, Arthur. *100 Years of Native American Painting*. Oklahoma City: The Oklahoma Museum of Art, 1978.

Snodgrass, Jeanne O. *American Indian Painters: A Biographical Directory*. New York: Museum of the American Indian; Heye Foundation, 1968.

Soustelle, Jacques. *The Olmecs: The Oldest Civilization in Mexico*. Trans. by Helen R. Lane. Norman: University of Oklahoma Press, 1985.

Suttles, Wayne. "Central Coast Salish." In *Volume 7, Handbook of North American Indians*, ed. by Wayne Suttles, 453-475. Washington D. C.: Smithsonian Institution, 1990.

Truettner, William H. *The Natural Man Observed: A Study of Catlin's Indian Gallery*. Washington, D.C.: Smithsonian Institution Press, 1979.

VanStone, James W. "Mainland Southwest Alaska Eskimo." In *Volume 5, Handbook of North American Indians*, ed. by David Damas, 224-242. Washington D. C.: Smithsonian Institution, 1984.

Wade, Edwin L., ed. *The Arts of the North American Indian: Native Traditions in Evolution*. New York: Hudson Hills Press, Inc., 1986.

Wade, Edwin L. "American Indian Paintings and Sculpture." In *The Philbrook Museum of Art: A Handbook to the Collections*. Ed. by Carol Haralson, 195-221. Tulsa: The Philbrook Museum of Art, 1991.

Wade, Edwin L. and Rennard Strickland. *Magic Images: Contemporary Native American Art*. Norman: Philbrook Art Center and University of Oklahoma Press, 1981.

Wardell, Allen. *Objects of Bright Promise: Northwest Coast Indian Art from the American Museum of Natural History*. Second edition revised. New York: American Federation for the Arts, 1988.

Wyckoff, Lydia L., ed. *Visions and Voices: Native American Painting From the Philbrook Museum of Art*. Albuquerque: University of New Mexico Press, 1996.